TELL ME MORE
ABOUT THE GOSPEL

Second edition (2012)
Bert Cargill

TELL ME MORE ABOUT THE GOSPEL

Second edition (2012)

Bert Cargill

JOHN RITCHIE LTD
CHRISTIAN PUBLICATIONS

40 Beansburn, Kilmarnock, Scotland

ISBN-13: 978-1-9040-6431-2

Copyright © 2013 by John Ritchie Ltd.
40 Beansburn, Kilmarnock, Scotland
www.ritchiechristianmedia.co.uk

Acknowledgements:

The author is grateful for the help given in the production of this book, especially from –

the Directors of John Ritchie Ltd for their encouragement, and their permission to adapt material from Foundation Truths of the Gospel by John Ritchie (1893);

Alan Park from Scotland, and at Luansha in Zambia, for helping to make the book more appropriate for Zambian readers;

believers in the Gospel Hall, East Road, Lusaka, Zambia, for reading part of the manuscript and advising where clarification was required;

Isobel, my wife and true helper, for her patience and constant support in this and many other similar projects;

Robert Smith and staff at Evangelical Mission Press, Bellville, South Africa, for advice and co-operation during the publication of the first edition.

Scripture quotations:

Throughout this book, Scripture quotations have been taken from the Authorised (King James) Version of the Bible, but with verb endings and a few obsolete words changed to promote clarity.

PREFACE

This book has been written for those who wish to learn more about the Gospel, the wonderful message from God which shows to us the way of salvation (Acts 16.17). Many years ago, the apostle Paul wrote to Christians in the city of Rome, "I am not ashamed of the Gospel of Christ: for it is the power of God unto salvation to every one who believes" (Romans 1.16). Since then, many others all over the world have believed the Gospel, as I trust you have done.

Perhaps some of you have only recently trusted Christ as your Saviour. To help you to benefit from this book, very little background knowledge of the Bible is assumed. However, the Bible is the authority for what we believe. It is important to know the verses in the Bible which tell us about the Gospel. From this book you can find where these verses are, and you should read them and note them. You can then refer to them when trying to explain the Gospel to others, either in personal conversation or public preaching. We must be sure that what we believe and what we teach is based upon the Word of God. Remember that it is "the Holy Scriptures which are able to make you wise to salvation through faith which is in Christ Jesus" (2 Timothy 3.15). The command to us today is the same as it was from Paul to Timothy: "Preach the Word" (2 Timothy 4.2).

Tell Me More About the Gospel has been designed especially and firstly for readers in many parts of the world whose native or local language is not English. Therefore the style of writing has been kept simple, avoiding difficult words and complicated sentences. Each chapter ends with a few questions with answers, some suggestions for further study to expand and revise the teaching of the chapter, and a short summary of the main points. A small amount of material has been repeated in some chapters to allow each to be read and studied on its own.

The book will of course be easy to understand by experienced readers of English and will be helpful to many of them also.

The idea for this book came from one which was written in 1893 by John Ritchie of Scotland, called Foundation Truths of the Gospel. He wrote for readers in the UK then, in a style of language which is not so easy to follow nowadays. The company which he founded and bears his name, has encouraged this fresh publication to serve a much wider readership.

The author acknowledges that a few parts of it are modified versions of what Mr Ritchie wrote these many years ago, to help those who had recently trusted Christ and wished to learn more about their salvation. He believed that it would deepen their understanding of the Gospel, and help them to live out in daily practice what they believed with all their hearts. This is the aim of this book also, and the prayerful desire of all who have been involved in its production.

* * * * *

This second edition has been produced in response to the interest in first edition of 2005. It has been extensively used throughout several African countries and also in other continents, having been translated into other languages including Bemba, Setswana, Armenian, Tamil and Sinhala. This new edition will be even easier to read and to translate. It includes some minor changes and a few additions, taking account of feedback received.

Bert Cargill
St Monans
Scotland
2012

Contents

CHAPTER 1

Introduction - The Gospel

Only One Gospel – What is it?

All we know about the Gospel is contained in the Bible. There is only one Gospel, the message from God which tells how He can save sinners. The word *'gospel'* means *'good news'*. Surely the message which has come from heaven to earth that God can save sinners is very good news!

It is based on what the Scriptures say, as we read in 1 Corinthians 15.1-4: "the gospel which I preached to you, which also you received, ... by which also you are saved, ... how that Christ died for our sins *according to the Scriptures*; and that He was buried, and that He rose again the third day *according to the Scriptures*".

These Old Testament scriptures promised that a Saviour would come. The New Testament shows how that promise was fulfilled as described in the four Gospels written by Matthew, Mark, Luke, and John. They record with great care different aspects of the birth and life, the service and teaching, the death, burial, and resurrection of our Lord Jesus Christ. The one great Gospel message is based upon what is recorded in these four Gospels.

This message is so important, that we should spend some time trying to learn more about it. This will help us to enjoy it all the more ourselves. It will also help us to tell it to others, and help us to defend it from attack. There are many enemies of the Gospel, and many false gospels which confuse people. In addition, it will lead us to worship and praise God even more as we understand more of what He has done.

The Gospel is the *greatest and best* message ever made known in this world -

- because it comes from God – the greatest authority in the universe;
- because it comes to us – everyone of us everywhere, the greatest number of people;
- because it is about the Lord Jesus Christ - the greatest Person ever;
- because it promises so much for those who believe it – the greatest of present and eternal blessings. But for those who reject or neglect it the consequences are great and very solemn and sad.

It is a message so *simple* that a child can receive it and benefit from it. But it is also so *profound* that those who know it best are always amazed at how deep and how wonderful it is. It is not a complicated and difficult message to understand, but its blessings are so many and so great that they will be known fully only when we get to heaven.

In this opening chapter of our book, let us now look at three ways in which the Gospel is described in the New Testament. Then in the chapters to follow, we can study in detail what it does for those who believe and receive it.

1. "The Gospel of God" (Romans 1.1)

God is the great *author and source* of the Gospel. He planned it, in His great love for the sinful men and women of this world. John 3.16 clearly shows this: "God so loved the world that He gave His only begotten Son ..." God also provided everything which was necessary to fulfil that plan. To provide for our salvation, "He spared not His Son but delivered Him up for us all" (Romans 8.32).

This is indeed most amazing, that it was man who sinned and yet it is God who has provided the means by which man can be saved.

- He provided all that His justice required for the punishment of sin.
- He provided all that His holiness demanded in His hatred of sin.
- He provided all that His grace would do in His love for sinners.

This plan of salvation was in place "before the foundation of the world" (1 Peter 1.20), and then when "the fulness of the time was come" (Galatians 4.4), "the Father sent the Son to be the Saviour of the world" (1 John 4.14). God's plan of salvation was in His mind and heart long before Adam sinned in the Garden of Eden and brought sin and death into the world. When Christ came, that plan was worked out and everything necessary for the salvation of our souls was done on the Cross at Calvary.

So the Gospel of God is a wonderful revelation of God Himself. It shows to us -

- His great eternal love (John 3.16; 1 John 4.10)
- His rich grace and mercy (Ephesians 1.7; 2.4-5; Acts 20.24)
- His perfect righteousness (Romans 1.17; 3.21-22)
- His mighty power (Romans 1.16; Ephesians 1.19-20)
- His amazing wisdom (Romans 11.33; Ephesians 3.10).

Only a wise and almighty God could provide a Gospel like this, and all the praise and glory belongs to Him (Ephesians 1.12).

2. "The Gospel of Christ" (Romans 1.16)

The Gospel is the Gospel of God *concerning His Son* (Romans 1.1, 3). The message itself is *about Christ and what He has done* to make it possible for us to be saved. He is ***the subject and the centre*** of this message of which God is the author and source.

Our salvation depends entirely upon the work of our Lord Jesus Christ, the Son of God. It is only by accepting what He has done, and by trusting in Him, that we can be saved. His death for sin and for sinners, His blood shed to redeem us, and His resurrection in victory over sin and death are the very foundation stones of the Gospel. Without all of these, we could never have been saved, but would still be in our sins (1 Corinthians 15.17).

Paul said, "We preach *Christ crucified*" (1 Corinthians 1.23). He also said, "We preach not ourselves, but *Christ Jesus the Lord*" (2 Corinthians 4.5). So this message is the *"Gospel of Christ"*. Any other gospel is false and misleading. Any message which says we must do something to improve ourselves is not the true Gospel of Christ. We could not do anything to earn salvation or to merit a blessing from God (Ephesians 2.8-9). Man is lost and ruined by sin, and cannot be saved apart from the work of Christ (Acts 4.12). Salvation must be accepted by faith as a gift from God (Romans 6.23).

The Gospel is based entirely on what the Bible teaches and depends entirely upon what Christ has done for us. "He bore our sins in His own body on the tree" (1 Peter 2.24). Only a Bible-based and Christ-centred message can be called the true Gospel. We should make this 'Good News' known in every possible way, out of love for Christ and a desire to see other people saved and blessed for eternity. We are to be "witnesses for Christ" in this world, wherever we are (Acts 1.8).

3 "The Gospel of your Salvation" (Ephesians 1.13)

The Gospel comes from God. It is about His Son, Christ Jesus. It is also a message for you and me, a message which meets man's deepest need. Wherever this message is preached and people believe it, they are saved from their sin. Whenever anyone trusts Christ, no matter who they are or what they have done, they receive salvation. Each believer can say that it is the gospel of *my* salvation, something **personal and precious**.

Believing the Gospel and trusting in the Lord Jesus makes a great difference in our life presently –

- instead of the guilt of sin we have joy and peace in believing (Romans 15.13);
- the love of God is in our hearts (Romans 5.5);
- we enjoy the presence of Christ and seek to serve Him now (Matthew 28.19-20).

Also our future outlook and our destiny are changed for ever - we are going to be in heaven (1 Peter 1.4), saved from hell and the lake of fire (Revelation 20.15).

There is no salvation apart from believing the Gospel. There is no Saviour apart from Christ Jesus the Lord (John 14.6). Everyone who has come in faith and called upon this Saviour has proved how true and effective the Gospel message really is. "*Whosoever* shall call upon the name of the Lord shall be saved" (Romans 10.13).

The reality of the Gospel has been known by many, many people throughout past centuries. It is also seen and enjoyed in the lives and experiences of many, many believers in different countries all over the world today.

- Are you one of them?
- Have *you* found that it is the "gospel of *your* salvation"?
- And are you helping to make it known to others?

QUESTIONS

1. What was the "gospel of the kingdom" which the Lord Jesus preached (Mark 1.14)?

He preached, "Repent and believe the gospel" (v.15). The people who believed His message and turned to follow Him became His disciples, accepting Him as their Saviour. The message was preached first to the nation of Israel (Matthew 10.6), but all who came to Him in faith He received and saved. Their sins were forgiven on the basis of His death which would soon take place.

Much of the Lord's teaching was about what He called "the kingdom". In this kingdom, Jesus Christ is Lord. All those who are born again are members of that kingdom (John 3.3,5). Christ rules in the hearts of those who accept Him as their Lord and Saviour now (Luke 17.21). In the future, Christ will return to earth and set up his millenial (one thousand years) kingdom. Then it will no longer be a kingdom hidden in the heart, but a visible one over all the earth (Revelation 11.15).

There is only one Gospel (Revelation 14.6), it is everlasting. It is only in and through Christ that men can be reconciled to God (John 14.6), and given eternal life (1Corinthians 15.22).

2. What does it mean to "evangelise"? Who are "evangelists"?

These words come from the Greek language in which the New Testament was written. The words mean "to announce good news" or "to preach the Gospel". So evangelists are those who use their time and efforts to make the Gospel known. Evangelising is telling out God's Good News. This is something which every believer should do.

FOR FURTHER STUDY

1. At least four things make the Gospel a great message, as you have read at the beginning of this chapter. Write them down and try to think of other ways in which the Gospel is great.

2. The word "Gospel" is used in two ways in the New Testament. Explain how there is only one Gospel, but there are also four Gospels.

3. Read Galatians 1.6-7 and explain what "another gospel" is. Why does Paul give such a strong rebuke to those who preach "another gospel"? (see v.9)

POINTS TO REMEMBER

- The word *'gospel'* means *'good news'*. There is only one Gospel, the message of God which tells how He can save sinners.
- The Gospel is based entirely on what the Bible teaches and depends entirely upon what Christ has done.
- God is the great **author and source** of the Gospel.
- The Lord Jesus Christ is **the subject and the centre** of the Gospel.
- The Gospel is something **personal and precious** to each person who believes.
- Each believer should always try to make the Gospel known to others.

18 TELL ME MORE ABOUT THE GOSPEL

CHAPTER 2

Saved

When someone believes in the Lord Jesus Christ and accepts the gift of eternal life, that person is saved immediately. Their sins are forgiven, and they are made ready for heaven. The only one who can save is the Lord Jesus Christ, as we read in Acts 4.12, "Neither is there salvation in any other: for there is no other name under heaven given among men, whereby we must be saved". Salvation is knowing that you are saved. It is the most important thing in life.

The Bible tells us at least five things about salvation.

1. Salvation is needed by everyone.
Everyone needs to be saved because everyone is lost, lost in sin. We are *all sinners* (Romans 3.23) who have chosen to go our own way instead of following God's way. That way is very dangerous now, and in the future it will end in the terrible judgement and punishment of hell for ever (Matthew 7.13-14). We need to be saved from present danger *and* from future judgement. We cannot save ourselves, for we are "without strength" (Romans 5.6). Without God, we are helpless and hopeless (Ephesians 2.12). If we are going to be saved, someone will need to come and find us and save us. We cannot find the way back to God by ourselves.

The good news of the Gospel is that "Christ Jesus came into the world *to save sinners*" (1 Timothy 1.15). The name Jesus was given to Him because it describes what He came to do: "He shall save His people from their sins" (Matthew 1.21). We often call Him the Saviour, or better "our Saviour" (Titus 2.13). He came to seek and to save those who were lost (Luke 19.10). The parables Jesus told in Luke 15 about the lost sheep, the lost coin, and the lost son beautifully describe how far the Saviour went to seek the lost sinner, and how much God wants the sinner to be found and saved. There is always wonderful joy in heaven over a sinner who repents and is saved. God does not want anyone to perish (2 Peter 3.9). He wants *everyone* to come to Christ and be saved (1 Timothy 2.4).

- No one is so good that they do not require salvation. Our own righteousness is like "filthy rags" in God's sight (Isaiah 64.6). Our best is not good enough for God to accept because it is far short of what He requires. Man's best is always stained by sin, perhaps by the sin of pride and boasting.

- No one is so bad that God cannot save them when they repent of their sin and accept Christ as Saviour. "The blood of Jesus Christ His Son, cleanses us from all sin" (1 John 1.7). The "chief of sinners" has been saved (1 Timothy 1.15).

The church, or any kind of religion, cannot save anyone. No priest or church official can give to anyone the salvation they need. Good works or prayers or penance cannot save. "Salvation belongs to the Lord" (Psalm 3.8; Jonah 2.9). "Apart from Me there is no Saviour," says God (Isaiah 43.11).

Salvation is a work which God does in the human soul. It is the combined work of the Father, the Son, and the Holy Spirit. It was planned by God the Father in heaven, worked out through Christ the Son on the Cross, and is applied by the Holy Spirit when someone repents and trusts in Christ.

2. Salvation is a gift from God.

No one deserves salvation. No one can earn it , or work to obtain it. "By *grace* are you saved through faith, and that not of yourselves; it is the *gift* of God: not of works, lest any man should boast" (Ephesians 2.8-9). "The *grace* of God that brings salvation has appeared to all men" (Titus 2.11).

God's grace is His kindness and love to those who deserve punishment rather than kindness. Romans 6.23 tells us that "The wages of sin is death" (this is what we all deserve) "but the *gift* of God is eternal life through Jesus Christ our Lord" (this is what we can receive by grace). God's mercy spares us from the punishment which our sins deserve. "According to His mercy He saved us" (Titus 3.5).

When God saves lost sinners by His grace, He has not ignored His own justice or set aside His own righteousness. The Cross of our Lord Jesus Christ shows us God's justice and His love. God's justice demanded that sin be punished by death. His love gave His Son to die instead of us. The death of that sinless One has made it possible for God's grace to reach sinners and take away our sin. We must always remember that the death of Christ is the basis for man's salvation.

3. Salvation is the message of the Gospel.

The Gospel of Christ is the power of God to bring *salvation* to every one who believes (Romans 1.16). God has sent this good news of salvation into the world to reach people everywhere - "to all nations" (Matthew 28.19; Romans 16.26).

- It is a message of invitation and welcome (Matthew 11.28).
- It is a call to repentance and change (Acts 2.38).
- It promises great blessing and eternal joy (Romans 5.1).
- It warns about the danger of neglecting or rejecting the message (Hebrews 2.3).

The Gospel must be preached right on to the end of this day of grace. It is a solemn responsibility for us to bring the Gospel message to others. It is also a great privilege for every Christian to make the Gospel known. Let us do so at every opportunity.

There is no restriction on the message - it is for "whosoever will" (Revelation 22.17). God has provided *salvation for all*, yet only those who heed the message and accept the Saviour will be saved. The alternative is condemnation and eternal loss: "He that does not believe is condemned already" (John 3.18-19).

4. Salvation is received by faith.

There is only one way to be saved. It is by faith - trusting in Christ Himself to save you. When the question was asked in the prison at Philippi long ago, "What must I *do* to be saved?" the reply was clear and simple, "*Believe* on the Lord Jesus Christ, and you will be saved" (Acts 16.30-31). The Lord Jesus said, "He that hears My word, and *believes* on Him that sent Me, has everlasting life" (John 5.24).

There is no other way to God. Jesus said, "I am the door: by Me if anyone enters in, he shall be saved" (John 10.9). It is a *step of faith* to enter in through the open door to be saved and to be safe for ever. To remain outside is to be lost.

5. Salvation is present and eternal.

Each believer can look back to a time in the *past* when by faith they accepted the Lord Jesus as their personal Saviour. That is when they *were saved*. Like Paul and Timothy, they can speak of God as the One "who *has* saved us" (2 Timothy 1.8). They are not now hoping to be saved, or waiting or praying to be saved. Here and now they have the "knowledge of salvation" (Luke 1.77) by believing what the Word of God has said. They know their sins are forgiven because they have believed (1 John 2.12). They know they can never be lost now or in the future because Christ has said so (John 10.28).

But salvation is also a *present* experience which continues every day. Romans 5.10 tells us that "much more being reconciled, we shall be saved by His life". Also we read, "He is able also to save them to the uttermost (to the very end) that come unto God by Him" (Hebrews 7.25). We are being *continually saved* by the Lord Jesus. We must resist sins and temptations while we live in this world, and so every day we need a Saviour. The risen Christ in heaven at God's right hand is our Advocate to ensure our acceptance by God (1 John 2.2). He is also our Great High Priest to help us through our temptations and trials (Hebrews 4.15-16).

The full completion of our salvation is *future*. "Now is our salvation nearer than when we believed" (Romans 13.11). "He shall appear the second time without sin, unto salvation" (Hebrews 10.27). At the second coming of the Lord Jesus, believers on earth, together with those who have died in Christ, will be glorified together (1 Thessalonians 4.16-17). Then in spirit, soul, and body, we shall inherit all that the Lord Jesus has prepared for them that love Him. We will enjoy salvation *for ever*.

If you are a believer, you can say that you *are saved*, you *are being saved*, and you *will be saved*.

- In the *past* you have been saved *from the penalty of sin* - on the Cross at Calvary Christ died to pay that penalty for you. Your sins have been forgiven.
- At *present* you are being saved *from the power of sin* - on the throne of heaven Christ lives to keep you safe. The power of sin over you has been broken.
- In the *future* you will be saved *from the presence of sin* - at the Lord's return believers will be removed from this sinful world altogether. We will live in His sinless presence for ever.

What a wonderful salvation!

QUESTIONS

1. *What does the text mean: "He that shall endure unto the end, the same shall be saved" (Matthew 24.13)?*

   When you read this verse along with the rest of Matthew 24, you will see that it refers to the people of Israel who will be on earth in the future, during a period of terrible suffering called "the great tribulation" (v. 21). The "end" is not the close of earthly life; nor is "saved" the salvation of a sinner from sin and hell. It is the rescue or salvation of the Jewish nation from their enemies on earth. The text does not refer to our salvation from sin.

2. *What does it mean to be "saved so as by fire" (1 Corinthians 3.15)?*

   This verse is about a believer and his reward being considered at the Judgement Seat of Christ. If that person has not lived for the Lord as he ought to have, the works of his life will not be worth anything for God's glory, and they will be burned up. He will lose his reward, but he will not lose his salvation. A good illustration of this is Lot who himself was saved out of Sodom, but his property and his works there were lost in the fire (Genesis 19).

3. *Is baptism necessary for salvation? Does Mark 16.16 teach this?*

   No, a person is saved when they put their trust in Christ. We are saved by faith, not works of any kind, not even good and commendable things such as baptism. The New Testament teaches that every one who is saved should after that be baptised in water to show in a public way that they belong to Christ. But baptism does not save anyone or fit them for heaven. Read the last part of Mark 16.16 carefully and you will see that those who are "condemned" (not saved), are those who *did not believe*. Baptism is not included as a necessary thing for salvation.

FOR FURTHER STUDY

1. Explain how the salvation of a soul depends upon the work of God the Father, God the Son, and God the Holy Spirit.

2. Note the meaning of past, present, and future salvation. Find the verses in the Bible which describe each of these.

3. What is the difference between God's grace and His mercy? Why are both required in our salvation?

4. We say that we cannot do anything to obtain salvation, but if a person just does nothing, that person will not be saved. Explain this. What *must* a person do to be saved?

5. Show how Romans 3.22 teaches that salvation is offered to all, but its great blessings do not come to all.

POINTS TO REMEMBER

- The Gospel message shows how we can be saved from sin and its punishment.

- Everyone needs to be saved. No one is so bad that they cannot be saved. No one is so good that they do not need to be saved.

- Salvation is a gift from God by His grace. It cannot be earned or deserved.

- There is only one Saviour and only one way to be saved, by faith in Christ Jesus.

- Salvation is a past decision, a present experience, and a future hope for every believer.

CHAPTER 3

Born Again

The Bible teaches that a person cannot be a Christian without being born again. This new birth is God's way of bringing people into His family when they are saved.

The Lord Jesus Christ Himself said, "You *must* be born again" (John 3.7). It is essential. He had also said in v.3, "Except a man be born again, he cannot see the kingdom of God." These words were first spoken to Nicodemus, a Jewish ruler who came to see Jesus one night long ago, but they are true for everyone.

To find out what the Bible says about the new birth, being "born again", we will need to read in John chapter 3 and in 1 Peter chapters 1 and 2, with references in some other Scriptures. We shall see this as we now consider what happens when someone is born again.

We are born into God's family.

Before we were saved we belonged to the family of man. There we were controlled by sin and Satan. We were fallen and sinful creatures who could not improve ourselves no matter how much we wanted to or tried to. This is what the Lord Jesus meant when He said, "That which is born of the flesh, is flesh" (John 3.6). We inherited our sinful nature (the flesh) from Adam through our parents, just as they had through their parents. So the sentence of death has been passed upon all the human race, "for all have sinned" (Romans 5.12). We also read that "in Adam all die" (1 Corinthians 15.22). By nature we were "children of wrath" (Ephesians 2.3).

God's way of dealing with the problem of our sinfulness was not to try to improve us, but to give us a completely new kind of life. This new life is spiritual, coming from God not man. It is eternal life, begun on earth but brought to us from heaven and fitting us for heaven. It is God's life, for we are brought into God's family - we become "children of God by faith in Christ Jesus" (Galatians 3.26).

We enter God's family by a spiritual birth in the same way as children enter a natural family by their physical birth. Birth is the only way to become part of a family, and once you are part of a family, you will always belong to it. So the life which God gives to His children is eternal and permanent.

When Nicodemus heard of being born again, he could not understand it. He could only think of natural birth from his mother. But Jesus showed him that to be saved and enter the kingdom of God, a spiritual experience was required, not a natural one.

The new birth makes us into a "new creation" (2 Corinthians 5.17). We are God's workmanship (Ephesians 2.10). A new man is formed in the image of God (Ephesians 4. 24; Colossians 3.10). When we are saved, a new life is given to us, but our old self is not removed from us.

So the born-again child of God has what are often called two 'natures', an old one from Adam and a new one from God. These are often called "the flesh" (the old one) and "the spirit" (the new one). There is often a struggle between these two natures in the believer. The old sinful desires which remain inside us pull us one way, to please ourselves; the Holy Spirit who is in us leads us the other way, to please God. We read about this struggle in Romans 6 and 7. In Galatians 5.16-17 we are told how to gain victory over the flesh and live how God wants us to live: "walk in the Spirit and you shall not fulfil the lust of the flesh".

We are born by God's Spirit.

Those who are born again receive the life of God *through the work of the Holy Spirit* who comes to dwell in them as soon as they are saved. So we are "born of the Spirit", Jesus said (John 3.8). **"It is the Spirit that gives life"** (John 6.63; 2 Corinthians 3.6). We also read that "He saved us, by the washing of regeneration and renewing of the Holy Spirit" (Titus 3.5).

The Holy Spirit works secretly and silently to give eternal life to those who are born again. The work of the Holy Spirit is like the wind, Jesus said. You can see its effects but you cannot tell where it comes from or where it goes (John 3.8). But you do see the change it makes. Likewise others should see a change when someone is born again, for they have "passed from death into life" (John 5.24).

It is God who gives life to each soul which was "dead in trespasses and sins" (Ephesians 2.1). Spiritual life cannot be obtained from any other source. The Lord Jesus said that those who become the children of God by believing on His name, were "born not of blood, nor of the will of the flesh, nor of the will of man, but of God" (John 1.13). This means that it cannot be passed on from a parent to a child within a human family.

Christian parents cannot pass on their salvation to their children. They want them to be saved and must earnestly pray for them, but each child must believe for themselves. Each must themselves be born again, born of God by the work of His Spirit.

We are born by God's Word.

In John 3.5 Jesus spoke of a person being born of water and of the Spirit. We have already seen how the Holy Spirit's work is essential for the new birth. But what does it mean to be born of "water"? First of all notice that this has nothing to do with baptism in water. When believers are baptised in water it is to give evidence to others that they already possess eternal life, not so that they might receive it.

To understand what water stands for here, we must think of what it meant to Nicodemus to whom it was first spoken. As a religious Jew he would recall that sometimes in the Old Testament water was a symbol of the Word of God, e.g., its cleansing power is described in Psalm 119.9 and in Psalm 51.2,7. Water is also frequently referred to in the New Testament in this way, e.g., Ephesians 5.25 describes "the washing of water by the Word", and in John 15.3 the Lord Jesus says, "You are clean through the Word which I have spoken to you."

When we read about the new birth later in the New Testament we find that the Word of God is definitely involved. 1 Peter 1.23 states, "Being born again, not of corruptible seed but of incorruptible, by the Word of God, which lives and abides for ever". James 1.18 states "Of His own will He begat us with the Word of truth".

Therefore a person is born again when they accept and **believe the Word of God**. That living seed takes root in their soul, and new life is begun by the work of the Holy Spirit. The Spirit works upon the Word to produce life. Without the Word, there would be nothing for the Spirit to work upon. That is why the exhortation to those who make the gospel known is to "Preach the Word!". "Faith comes by hearing and hearing by the Word of God" (Romans 10.17).

The water of God's Word must be applied to the heart and conscience to bring about conviction of sin and guilt. The Holy Spirit can then lead to repentance. The Word tells of Christ's power to save, and the Spirit leads to faith in Him.

The Spirit and the Word both point to Christ as Saviour. It is not ceremonies, sacraments, prayers or penance that saves. It is faith in Christ alone, faith which is based upon the truth of the Word of God made real by the Holy Spirit.

Conclusion

The testimony of the Scriptures is as follows: "Ye are all the children of God by *faith* in Christ Jesus" (Galatians 3.26); "Whosoever *believes* that Jesus is the Christ *is born of God*" (1 John 5.1); "Whosoever *believes* in Him should not perish, but *have eternal life*" (John 3.15).

Faith believes and receives the testimony of the Word of God. Faith looks to Christ and relies on Him alone. It does not look inside for evidences or feelings. It does not look outside for signs or miracles. The miracle of the new birth happens inside those who receive eternal life by faith.

Born of God, born of the Spirit, born by the Word of God - the believer is not re-formed outwardly, but a new life with a new nature is placed inside his or her mortal body. That new nature now begins to become evident through the believer's actions and attitudes. Other people will begin to see this. "In this the children of God are *manifest*" (1 John 3.10). "Whosoever is begotten of God does not sin" (that is, does not practise sin as a habit) (1 John 3.9). The members (parts) of our bodies, once the servants of sin, are now to be controlled by the new life. They are now used as "instruments of righteousness unto God" with the promise of "fruit unto holiness" (Romans 6.13,22).

QUESTIONS

1. *Is it necessary for a believer to be able to give the day and date of his or her second birth?*

In the lifetime of every true child of God there certainly must have been a moment when they began their spiritual life as a child of God, just as there was a moment when they began their natural life as a child of their parents. That was the moment of their second birth. Most believers can remember when it happened. But to say that everyone must know that moment exactly, and be able to point to the day and date and time, would be going beyond what the Scriptures require.

But there *must* be a new and heavenly birth, a new beginning. It is not a gradual transition or an evolution from the old towards the new. In the natural world and in the spiritual world, what we see is creation, not evolution. Evolution is a theory of men; creation is the work of God.

2. *Is it correct to speak about being a "born again Christian"?*

If a person is a Christian they have been born again, and if they are not born again they are not a Christian at all in the Bible sense of that word. It is not necessary to use both terms together. (It is like speaking about a "male man".) The disciples of the Lord Jesus were first called Christians at Antioch (Acts 11.26), and no other extra name was required to describe them.

Sadly today, however, many who have never been saved call themselves "Christian" - it is just a profession. Because of this some people have added the term "born again" to emphasise that they are true believers in Christ.

FOR FURTHER STUDY

1. 'Regeneration' is a word often used to describe the new birth. In what ways does regeneration differ from reformation?

2. Reincarnation is a false and misleading idea in which some people believe that a person has lived on earth before, perhaps in some different form, and then is living their life over again. This is **not** what being born again means. Read Hebrews 9.27 and see how the Bible tells us that reincarnation is a false belief.

3. Read John 16.7-15, and write down the things which the Lord Jesus said the Holy Spirit would do in the world, and in the hearts of believers.

4. What do new born babies need to make them grow and develop? Read 1 Peter 2.2-3 and note how this applies to your growth as a child of God. Make a list of other things which reading God's Word will do for you.

POINTS TO REMEMBER

- No one can enter God's family or be in the kingdom of God without being born again.
- The new birth is a spiritual experience, not a natural one. It happens only once.
- Being born again means to be brought into a life which is new and different.
- The Holy Spirit of God gives eternal life to those who are born again.
- The Word of God is essential to the new birth, to bring about repentance for sin and faith in Christ.
- Those who are born again will grow up into a mature Christian life only by feeding on the Word of God.

CHAPTER 4

Converted

When a person trusts in the Lord Jesus and is born again, a wonderful change takes place. God gives to them a new, spiritual life in their soul. The change is called conversion, which means to be turned round into a new and different direction.

This change is inward and complete, not just partial or outward on the surface. It is permanent, for ever, not just temporary, for a short time.

- It is turning to Christ - away from sin and Satan.
- It is turning to God - from false idols of any kind.
- It is turning to cleanness and holiness - away from the world and its wicked ways.

This change is inward but it will be shown outwardly in the daily life of the person who has been converted.

The Bible teaches us the following things about conversion.

1. Conversion is necessary.

The Lord Jesus said, "Except you be *converted,* and become as little children, you shall not enter into the kingdom of heaven" (Matthew 18.3). The early apostles preached the same message: "Repent therefore and be *converted* that your sins may be blotted out" (Acts 3.19).

To find the way of salvation, everyone must turn from the way they are on, because that way is wrong: "All we like sheep have gone astray; we have turned every one to his own way" (Isaiah 53.6). Man's face is naturally turned away from God his Creator, on a path that leads down to death and hell. In Romans 3.11-12 we read "none seek after God; they are all gone out of the way". So a change of mind and heart is necessary, turning away from sin and self and turning towards God and the Lord Jesus Christ. The word the Bible uses for this change is 'repentance'.

The Lord is calling today as He did long ago, "*Turn* from your evil ways; for why will you die?" (Ezekiel 33.11). Similarly we read in Isaiah 55.6-7: "Seek ye the Lord while He may be found, call upon Him while He is near: let the wicked forsake his way and the unrighteous man his thoughts: and let him *return* to the Lord, and He will have mercy upon him."

The Gospel message is "repentance toward God and faith toward our Lord Jesus Christ" (Acts 20.21). If a sinner repents and trusts in the Lord Jesus that sinner will be converted.

2. Conversion is fundamental.

Conversion is not a change of religion. It is not joining a new church, or trying a new theology. It is not just a correction of bad habits. It is not making good resolutions or taking new vows and making a fresh start. Many people try this without coming to Christ in repentance and faith. They do not continue because their heart has not been touched and changed inside.

Conversion is a real turning to God. "You *turned to* God from idols" (1 Thessalonians 1.9). "You are now *returned* to the Shepherd and Bishop of your souls" (1 Peter 2.24). It is a real and radical change.

- The heart which was once closed against God's love is now opened to receive it, as a flower turns towards the sun to receive its heat and light.

- The ear once closed against God's voice, is now ope His Word.

- The mind and heart which wanted its own way now wishes to go God's way and do His will.

- The power of sin and Satan is now replaced by the power of grace and the power of the Holy Spirit to influence and control a believer.

The person is brought "from darkness to light, and from the power of Satan unto God" (Acts 26.18). "Old things are passed away; behold all things are become new" (2 Corinthians 5.17).

3. Conversion is the work of God.

We cannot convert ourselves: *only God can convert us*. We noted in the last chapter what it means to be born again. When we are born again, it is God who gives us a new life and a new nature. He makes us "a new creation" (2 Corinthians 5.17). That is how He does the work of conversion in our souls. "The law of the Lord is perfect, converting the soul" (Psalm 19.7).

When we are converted, we will want to serve God and worship Him. The believers in Thessalonica had "turned to God from idols to serve the living and true God; and to wait for His Son from heaven" (1 Thessalonians 1.9-10). The power of idols was broken by the power of God. When they believed and received the living Christ as Saviour, their lives were really changed.

Naturally, man does not want to turn to God. But when people are convicted of sin and feel their guilt before God, they will be glad to turn to Him for salvation. Salvation from sin and guilt cannot be found anywhere else.

4. Conversion means changed behaviour.

It is always the same in the New Testament. Wherever the gospel message was received, there were those who "believed, and *turned to* the Lord" (Acts 11.21). Sadly some turned away from the offer of salvation and life and continued in their sin, but many others turned to Christ and received Him as Saviour.

Great changes were seen in their lives. At Ephesus, their old ways of witchcraft and superstition were abandoned, and their books were burned (Acts 19.19). At Philippi the converted jailor kindly cared for God's servants whom he had roughly put into prison a few hours before (Acts 16.33). Only God working in these people's lives could bring about such a radical change.

When Christ is received into the heart of a believer, the whole way of life is changed. "The love of Christ constrains us" to *do* what we could not do before and to *be* what He wants us to be now (2 Corinthians 5.14-15). Our friends, family and neighbours should see some real changes in us when we are converted.

5. Conversion is opposed by Satan.

Satan always tries to hinder the divine work of conversion. He "blinds the minds of them that believe not, to prevent the light of the glorious gospel of Christ shining into them" (2 Corinthians 4.4). He closes their eyes, he shuts their ears, he hardens their hearts to prevent them from "seeing and hearing and understanding and being converted" (Acts 28.27). Satan fears the Gospel of God, and so he tries to spread confusion by introducing other gospels which are false (Galatians 1.6-9).

The servants of Satan seek to turn away the ears of those who would hear the truth, as Elymas the sorcerer did in Acts 13.8. Satan also uses religious men with a form of godliness to deceive others with their false teachings (2 Timothy 3.5-8). They turn their hearers away from the truth to "fables" (4.3-4). Many such "fables" exist everywhere. These are false gospels which deny the sinfulness of man, the deity of Christ, the need for repentance, and salvation by faith alone. These false gospels tell people that they must do something to merit God's favour. The Bible tells us that we can never work or pay or do anything to earn salvation.

What should we do about these false teachings? We must "Preach the Word" (2 Timothy 4.2). This command of Paul to Timothy when false teachings were spreading is still the command of the Lord for us today. The Lord Jesus Himself commanded us to "go and preach the gospel" (Mark 16.15). Those who know the Gospel of God, having experienced its effects in their own lives, should be always ready to make it known in all its simplicity, freshness, and power. God will use His Word by His Spirit to convert others to Himself when they come in repentance and faith.

It is important to remember that although Satan opposes the Gospel and those who make it known, the power of God is always greater. We are saved by the power of God (1 Corinthians 1.18). He is the one who delivers us from Satan's power (Colossians 1.13). No one can say, "I could have been saved but the power of the devil was too great." That would be a vain excuse for failing to trust Christ for salvation.

All men and women will have to give account to God for their own decisions and actions. An example of this is Judas Iscariot. He fulfilled the plan of the devil, and also the prophecy of Scripture when he betrayed the Lord Jesus, but he was held accountable for what he did and went to "his own place" after he died (Mark 14.21; Acts 1.25).

QUESTIONS

1. *What did the Lord mean by saying to Peter, "When you are converted, strengthen your brethren" (Luke 22.32)? Was Peter not converted before?*

Yes, he was converted on the day he fell at Jesus' feet confessing his sinfulness (Luke 5.8). He left his old life and began to follow Jesus as a faithful disciple. But now Peter was about to be attacked by Satan, and the Lord knew he would fail. He failed when he denied his Lord three times. The Lord spoke these words with his *restoration* in view. After many bitter tears, and again at Jesus' feet, Peter was forgiven and restored to fellowship with Christ and with his brethren. Also he did strengthen them. We see this when we read the early chapters of Acts and read Peter's two epistles.

We can be saved (or born again) only once; but often we may require to be turned from a path of disobedience and failure in the way in which Peter was. In Luke 22.32 "converted" does not refer to the new birth which happens only once. It refers to the time when Peter would be turned again into the right path.

2. *What does repentance mean?*

Repentance is a complete change of mind and heart. It is not just being sorry for your sins, as someone might be because they are found out doing something wrong, or are about to be punished. Judas Iscariot was like that, but he never really changed inwardly.

Repentance is agreeing with God about your sin, about how your sin has offended God and rebelled against His laws, agreeing that His sentence and punishment is just. It is turning away from sin and making a break with the past life of disobedience to God. Read Psalm 51 and you will find out what true repentance involves. There we read how much David hates his sin, but he also hates himself for sinning, and casts himself on the mercy of God to be forgiven.

FOR FURTHER STUDY

1. Make a list of things which a person *turns from* when they are converted.

2. Make a list of things which a person *turns to* when they are converted.

3. Read the story about the healing of the mad man (Legion) in Mark 5.1-20. Notice how he is described in v.2-5, then in v.15 and v.18-20 after Jesus had healed him. Show how this great change is a picture of what happens to us at conversion, and illustrates the five main points in this chapter.

4. What does "a new creation" mean (2 Corinthians 5.17)?

POINTS TO REMEMBER

- Conversion is necessary for a person to become a Christian.
- Conversion is not trying a new religion or trying to become better.
- Conversion is a work which God does in a person's life when they accept Christ as Saviour.
- Conversion is an inward change which will be shown outwardly in daily life.
- Conversion means turning to God away from all that is sinful.
- The devil tries every possible way to hinder a person from being converted.
- Every person must decide for themselves to be saved from sin and converted to God.

CHAPTER 5

Redeemed

Twice in the New Testament we read these words about the Lord Jesus: "in whom we have redemption through His blood, the forgiveness of sins" (Ephesians 1.7; Colossians 1.14). This means that for us to be forgiven and brought to God, the Lord Jesus Christ had to pay a price. The price was His precious blood, to redeem us and set us free from sin. This great cost of our salvation is called our *redemption*.

To *redeem* means to buy back *someone or something which belongs to someone else*. The person who pays the price is called the Redeemer. Our Redeemer is the Lord Jesus Christ. 1 Peter 1.18-19 tells us that we have been redeemed with the precious blood of Christ. We once belonged to sin and Satan but now we belong to Him. We enjoy redemption through His blood. Those who are bought in this way are called the Redeemed. This is another lovely name for those who have been saved.

Why do we need to be redeemed?

Many years ago it was the custom for men and women in many parts of the world to be bought and sold as slaves. Some examples of this are found in the Bible, such as Joseph (Genesis 39.1), and the Israelites in Egypt (Exodus 1.11-14). Slaves belonged to their master, and could not do anything to obtain their freedom. They could only be set free if someone paid to their master the price he required for them, and then gave them their liberty.

The Bible teaches us that men and women are the **slaves of sin and Satan**. This started when man disobeyed God in the Garden of Eden and surrendered himself into Satan's power. Satan is now the "prince of this world" (John 12.31), and mankind is held in his power (Acts 26.18). Paul spoke of himself as being "sold under sin" (Romans 7.14). Jesus said that those who commit sin are "the slaves of sin" (John 8.34). All our lifetime we are subject to this bondage and slavery (Hebrews 2.15). This is why we need to be redeemed.

The Bible also tells us that no one can redeem himself, or redeem anyone else: "None of them can, by any means, redeem his brother, nor give to God a ransom for him" (Psalm 49.7). If we are going to be redeemed, God must do it for us. It is wonderful to hear God saying, "Deliver him from going down to the pit: I have found a ransom" (Job 33.24). Only God could provide that great ransom price which was required. Christ Jesus our Lord has obtained "eternal redemption" for His people (Hebrews 9.12). The only way to escape from the power of sin and Satan is to be delivered by the power of God.

What was the price of our redemption?

The price to be paid for redemption is called the *ransom*. This gives to the new owner the legal right to take possession of what he has purchased. There could be no redemption without the ransom price first being paid.

The ransom price for us was very great - "the man Christ Jesus who gave Himself a ransom for all" (1 Timothy 2.5-6). By this ransom, the Lord Jesus has obtained the legal right to everything in earth and heaven. Those who accept the salvation and deliverance which He offers, now belong to Him. They are redeemed. Notice that the ransom price has been paid for everyone, but only those who believe in Christ and accept His offer of salvation actually belong to Him. Only they enjoy the blessings of redemption and are freed from the power of sin.

The price could not have been paid in this world's money, which often changes and loses its value. The price was not "silver and gold" but *"the precious blood of Christ"* which has eternal value and power (1 Peter 1.18-19). We can say, "In whom we have redemption through

His blood, the forgiveness of sins, according to the riches of His grace" (Ephesians 1.7). Those who are redeemed belong to "the church of God which He purchased with His own blood" (Acts 20.28). Let us never forget how much it cost to redeem us from the power of sin and of Satan so that we could belong to God.

How could we be redeemed?

The whole human race was under the influence and power of Satan, so how could they be redeemed? How could God pay the ransom which was required? He did it by becoming man Himself. Our Lord Jesus Christ, the Son of God took a body of flesh and blood. Through His virgin birth, followed by His perfect sinless life, and then by His death on the cross that great price of redemption was paid.

The Old Testament shows us what a redeemer had to be and what he had to do. The Hebrew word for Redeemer is sometimes translated as "Kinsman" (or "Blood Relative") and also "Avenger". So it has a threefold meaning - *Kinsman, Redeemer, Avenger.* The Lord Jesus became our Kinsman, our Redeemer, and our Avenger.

Kinsman: Under the law, a kinsman, that is a blood relative, had a right to redeem and take possession of his brother's property after his death (Leviticus 25.25; Ruth 4.6-7). The Lord Jesus became our Kinsman by His incarnation. "Forasmuch then as the children are partakers of flesh and blood, He also Himself likewise took part of the same" (Hebrews 2.14). "He was made in the likeness of men" (Philippians 2.7). But His humanity was sinless. He had no share in man's fallen nature. In all respects except sin He was a real man. Thus He became our Kinsman. But that in itself was not enough to deliver us. The Lord Jesus became Kinsman so that He might become Redeemer.

Redeemer: Our redemption required the blood of Christ and the power of God. Redemption by blood and redemption by power are seen in Israel's deliverance from slavery in Egypt in Exodus 12 - 14. You should read Exodus 12 to see how they were redeemed by the blood of the lamb from the judgment of God which fell on Egypt. The blood protected them from that judgement. Then the power of the Lord saved and delivered them from Pharaoh who pursued them to the Red Sea. After they were safely across He destroyed their enemies in the sea. He "redeemed them from the hand of the enemy" (Psalm 106.10) so that they could become a special people for Himself (Exodus 19.5). Our redemption was by the precious blood shed on the cross, and by the great power of God made known at our Lord's resurrection. He has made us His special people (Titus 2.14).

Avenger: In the Old Testament, if a man's brother was murdered he was allowed to avenge the death of that brother on the one who had killed him (Joshua 20.5). In His death the Lord Jesus became our Avenger - "He destroyed him that had the power of death, that is the devil" (Hebrews 2.14). He 'bruised the serpent's head', fulfilling the great promise of Genesis 3.15. Because of His triumph over the enemy then, His people will see Satan bruised under their feet also in a future day (Romans 16.20).

What are the results of being redeemed?

A slave who has been redeemed starts a new life. From that point onwards things are different. Here are some of the changes which a Christian experiences after being redeemed.

Released from the power of darkness:

We no longer live under the rule and authority of the devil. We now live under the rule and authority of Christ. We have been transferred *out of the kingdom of darkness* into the kingdom of God's Son (Colossians 1:13-14, Acts 26:18).

Released from the power of sin:

We are also redeemed from the power of sin: Christ "gave Himself for us, that He might redeem us *from all iniquity*, and purify unto Himself a peculiar people, zealous of good works" (Titus 2.14). Our bodies should no longer be used for sinning. We should use them as instruments of righteousness for God (Romans 6.13). Sin no longer has power over us, so we should not live as if sin controlled us (Romans 6.14). We still have a sinful nature, and that means that we will occasionally sin, but this will not be our habit. God's desire is that we should not sin, but if we do sin, the Lord Jesus Christ is our Advocate to represent us before the Father so that we may be forgiven (1 John 1.9-10; 2:1-2).

Released from the curse of the law:

We are no longer under the curse of the law which we have broken, for "Christ has redeemed us *from the curse of the law*, being made a curse for us" (Galatians 3.13). The law cannot condemn us now (Romans 8:1-3). Christ willingly died in our stead, so that we who were once under the condemning curse of the law can be blessed instead.

Belonging to God:

We have changed owners (see 1 Corinthians 6.20). We have been *bought with a price*, so we should glorify God in our body and in our spirit which are God's. This will show to others that we do belong to Him. He is the best of Masters to belong to – so different from our old one, Satan.

Redemption of the body which will take place in the future:

The believer has been redeemed now, but there is also another part of redemption which is future. We are waiting for the adoption, that is, the "redemption of our body" (Romans 8.23). Our bodies have not yet been delivered from that condition into which sin brought them. It is still, "the body of our humiliation" (Philippians 3.20), which means that it gets old and tired and sick. It must either be "dissolved" - as it is in those who die (2 Corinthians 5.1); or it will be "changed" - as it will be in those who are "alive and remain" until the coming of the Lord (1 Corinthians 15.51; 1 Thessalonians 4.17). When He comes we shall be changed. We will receive a body which shall be *"like unto His glorious body"* (Philippians 3.20). We will then experience the fullness of redemption. Meantime we know that we are "sealed with that Holy Spirit of promise, which is the earnest (guarantee) of our inheritance, until the redemption of the purchased possession" (Ephesians 1.13-14).

God's work of redemption includes the whole of creation. For a long time all creation has been subject to the "bondage of corruption" (Romans 8.21). The earth was cursed by God in Genesis 3.17. It has been waiting for the time when it too shall be delivered and become a sharer in "the glorious liberty of the children of God" (Romans 8.20-23). Then a new heaven and a new earth shall be established, in which righteousness dwells for ever. Everything in that new creation shall continue in the power of redemption.

Through Christ and His redemption, God shall receive to Himself the glory lost by sin. Heaven will be filled with a redeemed people who will for ever sing to their Redeemer, the Lamb "in the midst of the throne", "Thou art worthy . . . for Thou wast slain, and hast redeemed us to God by Thy blood" (Revelation 5.6,9).

QUESTIONS

1. *Is it Scriptural to speak of all men as being redeemed?*

   No! Scripture does not say this. The death of Christ was for all, both people and things (2 Corinthians 5.14; Hebrews 2.9), but redemption includes deliverance. Unconverted men and women have not experienced this. The "redeemed of the Lord" are His people only. Those who reject the Redeemer and despise the Gospel will die in their sins.

2. *Are our bodies redeemed now?*

   Our bodies belong to God now (1 Corinthians 6.20), but the "full redemption" of the body will not happen until the Lord Jesus comes again (Romans 8.23). Sin once held us as slaves and our members were tools for doing Satan's work. But they belong to him no longer. "Now being made free from sin, we have become servants to God" (Romans 6.22). Those who are redeemed use their bodies and minds now on earth to serve God, while we wait for full redemption in heaven.

FOR FURTHER STUDY

1. After God delivered the children of Israel out of Egypt, the redemption of the first born, of man and of cattle, became necessary even when they reached the land of Canaan. Read Exodus 13.13-15 and see how important this was. In what ways can we be constantly reminded of our redemption?

2. Read Isaiah 49.24-26 and you will get another good picture of the work of a redeemer.

3. Psalm 107.1-3 tells the redeemed what to do and why. Do you do that? Find the four verses repeated in this Psalm which tell us what to do and when.

POINTS TO REMEMBER

*   Redemption is the purchase of our souls to God by the ransom price paid in the precious blood of Christ on the cross.
*   We had to be redeemed because Satan had us in his power due to our sinful nature and practices.
*   For us to be redeemed, the Son of God had to become a man, our "kinsman redeemer".
*   Redemption means we have been set free from the power of darkness (the mastery of Satan), from the power of sin, and from the curse of the law.
*   We now belong to God and should use our bodies and minds to serve and glorify Him.
*   In the future, the full blessings of redemption will give us bodies of glory like Christ's in heaven.
*   Then the blessings of redemption will benefit all creation also, when the curse is removed and everything will be made new and perfect again.

CHAPTER 6

Justified

In the New Testament, especially in the book of Romans, we read about being justified, for example in ch.5 v.1: "Being justified by faith, we have peace with God through our Lord Jesus Christ". This great truth of justification is important to understand.

- **Justification** is the act of God when He **declares as righteous** a sinner who has trusted in the Lord Jesus for salvation. He justifies us when we are saved.
- The work of **making** that sinner into a righteous person is called **sanctification**. We will consider this subject later, that is how our behaviour is changed after we are saved.

The Gospel message tells us how a righteous God can accept a guilty sinner who deserves only condemnation and punishment. God declares that the sinner is righteous when he or she trusts in Jesus Christ to save them. If you are justified it means that God has declared that you are righteous (or just) in His sight.

We now look at five things the Bible says about our justification.

1. "It is God that Justifies" (Romans 8.33)
In the Old Testament the question was asked, "How then can man be justified with God?" (Job 25.4). We need forgiveness for our sins, but God does more than that! He actually takes away every accusation of sin brought against us, and declares us righteous in His sight. He changes our position before Him from "condemnation" to "justification" (Romans 8.1).

In a court of law, a person may be found guilty, but for special reasons may be pardoned, and thus spared from the penalty of the law. But the person is still guilty. It would have been much better if the guilt had also been taken away. That is what justification does, and **only God can do it**. We do not become innocent, but rather that being guilty sinners, we are declared righteous by the highest authority possible, by God Himself.

God declares and treats as righteous those who put their trust in Christ. Two things then follow:

(1) no punishment for sin is now required;

(2) no one can accuse the sinner any more.

God has changed the whole situation. It is wonderful how sinners can now stand in God's holy presence and be seen by God as though they had never sinned at all. So the questions asked in Romans 8.33-34 are quickly answered:

(1) "Who shall lay anything to the charge of God's elect?" No one can, because God Himself has justified them.

(2) "Who is he that condemns?" No one can, because Christ has died and borne the judgement of the sinner's sin.

God credits (imputes) righteousness to those who put their faith in Christ (Romans 4.23-24). From then on they are "in Christ". God treats them as righteous because Christ's righteousness has been credited to them. His righteousness is perfect. We could never be righteous in ourselves. Human righteousness is incomplete and faulty. Here is what the Bible states: "There is none righteous, no, not one" (Romans 3.10). "All our righteousnesses are as filthy rags" (Isaiah 64.6). Yet some people still "go about to establish their own righteousness" and will not accept "the righteousness of God" (Romans 10.3).

God Himself declares His own righteousness in the cross of Christ (Romans 3.24-25). Because of what Christ did on that cross, God can be just, and the justifier of those who believe in Jesus (Romans 3.26). The just Judge is the justifier! The righteous God declares that the sinner is righteous!

2. "Justified by His Blood" (Romans 5.9)

Since God is just, the penalty of sin must be paid. A holy God could not overlook or excuse sin. So Christ came, and He, the Just One, took upon Himself the sins of us who are the unjust ones (1 Peter 3.18). "He made Him to be sin for us, who knew no sin, that we might be made the righteousness of God in Him" (2 Corinthians 5.21). Our Lord Jesus was made an offering for sin so that we could be justified. Personally, Christ had no sin of His own, but He bore the judgement for our sins. Personally, the believer has no righteousness, but is reckoned "righteous … in Him". We could never be justified apart from the work of our Lord Jesus Christ on the cross.

Justification is only possible because of the **shed blood of Christ**. His death on the cross provided what God required and what man needed.

- His death provided what *God required* for righteousness and justice - sin's penalty has been paid.
- His death also provides what the *sinner need*s for salvation and justification - we can be "justified freely by His grace through the redemption that is in Christ Jesus" (Romans 3.24).

Justification is thus the result of redemption. In the chapter about redemption we saw how the price was paid and the work completed. Sin's penalty had to be paid in blood, "the precious blood of Christ as of a lamb without blemish and without spot" (1 Peter 1.19). God's righteousness would have to be satisfied before His grace could be shown. So we read that "mercy and truth are met together; righteousness and peace have kissed each other" (Psalm 85.10). All this happened at the cross of Christ.

3. "Justified by His Grace" (Romans 3.24)

The source of justification is the love of God for us. It was His love which planned and provided for us to be saved, redeemed, and justified. There was nothing in us or about us which could ever merit salvation, or cause God to look favourably upon us. We are justified by His grace - in spite of the fact that we were guilty sinners. We did not deserve to be treated kindly.

But *God makes His grace available to all* - all who "have sinned and come short of the glory of God" (Romans 3.23). No one is good enough to deserve it, and no one is too bad to be beyond it. God justifies "the ungodly" (Romans 4.5) by His grace. When a sinner comes to God for salvation, he or she must come just as they are, and everyone who comes in faith is "justified freely by His grace".

God's *grace* gives us what we never could deserve: He justifies us, makes us His children and gives us eternal life. At the same time God's *mercy* keeps back what we do deserve, that is punishment for our sins. He saves us in His mercy and by His grace. He gives salvation to those who deserve judgement.

4. "Justified by Faith" (Romans 5.1)

- God can justify the sinner because the blood of Christ has been shed.
- We can be justified because God is a God of grace.
- We obtain justification by our faith in Christ. It cannot be obtained in any other way.

God has always blessed those who have trusted Him. In Romans 4, we read how the faith of Abraham and the faith of David brought them into blessing and favour with God. Hebrews 11 tells of many others who were commended for their faith. So for us today, the wonderful blessing of justification comes by faith. We read in Acts 13.39, "All that *believe* are justified".

This is the only way in which we can obtain justification - by faith in God, by trusting Christ as Saviour. It is the same message in Ephesians 2.8-9: "By grace you are saved *through faith*, and that not of yourselves; it is the gift of God, not of works, lest anyone should boast". We are told that "by the deeds of the law no flesh can be justified in God's sight" (Romans 3.20). Because it is by faith, anyone may have it, the young or the old, the poor or the rich, the sick and the healthy - anyone can put their faith in God and be justified.

The work of the Cross was *for all*, and God's grace is offered *to all*, so why is justification not possessed *by all*? - simply because all do not believe. Some receive the Saviour and are saved by God's grace, but others reject Him. Some "believe" the testimony of God, and some "believe not" (Acts 28.24). It is "*unto all*" (offered to all and available to all), but it is only "*upon all them that believe*" (given to them that believe) (Romans 3.22). Unbelievers refuse or reject the provision God has made, and never benefit from it.

5. "Justified by Works" (James 2.24)

In the Epistle of James, another aspect of justification is described. It is different from what Romans has described. In Romans, justification by faith is the subject. This is what God sees, giving to the believer the righteousness which God requires. This righteousness can never be obtained by working for it - it is the gift of grace accepted by faith as we have seen.

Now we read in James 2.24 that "*by works* a man is justified, and not by faith only". Also, "Was not Abraham our father justified *by works* when he had offered up his son upon the altar?" (James 2. 21). What Abraham did was an *evidence* of his faith. He would not have offered up Isaac if He had not first believed God. So his faith was *shown* by his works. In Romans 4 we learn about Abraham being justified *by faith*, but his works are not spoken about. In James 2 we learn about his *works*, because what he did was an important evidence of his faith.

We cannot see another person's faith. We can only see the evidence of their faith, what is done outwardly. Works are the outward evidence of inward faith.

- We are justified by *faith before God*.
- We are justified by *works before men*.

God alone knows our heart, but we must show to others the evidence of our faith. It will be seen in what we do and how we live. We were not saved by working for our salvation, but once saved we will do things which show how real our faith is. The grace which saves us teaches us "that denying ungodliness and worldly lusts, we should live soberly, righteously, and godly, in this present world" (Titus 2.12). Those who "say" they have faith must "show" it by their works (James 2.18).

QUESTIONS

1. *If the believer is justified from all things (Acts 13.39), why do we have to "confess our sins" (1 John 1.9)?*

   Justification is a legal term, and shows God in His character as Judge. The sinner is justified once for all, declared righteous by God in His courts. That act is never repeated. But God is also the Father of His children. If, as a child, he disobeys his Father, fellowship will be broken and unhappiness will be the result. The only way to be restored is by confession of the sin. When we confess, our Father forgives, and fellowship is enjoyed again. It is not a question of judgement but of fellowship and enjoyment.

   Suppose that a judge in a court of justice, after dealing with all the criminal cases for the day, goes home to find that his own child has been disobedient or unruly during the day. He does not then take the place of a judge, or 'try' the case by the rule of the criminal law. He has another rule for his home, that of parental authority. He deals with the disobedient child as a father and not as a judge in the court giving out the law's sentence to a criminal. In the same way God is the Judge of the world; He is the Father of His children.

2. *What does it mean when we read that "He was raised again for our justification" (Romans 4.25)?*

   The blood of Christ shed on the cross laid the basis for our justification. If He had not died for us, it would not have been possible for God to justify us. The resurrection of Christ is the assurance that God has fully accepted all the work done on the cross. If He had not risen from the dead, there would have been no hope of forgiveness of sins and peace with God (1 Corinthians 15.17). Christ's resurrection is the guarantee that our justification is real.

FOR FURTHER STUDY

1. We read in Romans 3.4 that God is justified in His sayings, and in 1 Timothy 3.16 that Christ was justified in the spirit. Explain how the exact meaning of "justification" helps us to understand what this means.

2. Proverbs 17.15 and 24.24 say that it is wrong to justify the wicked. How is this different from the truth of justification by faith?

3. Explain how God is "Just" and the "Justifier" of those who believe in Jesus (Romans 3.26).

4. Explain how justification takes place in an instant, and is complete, final, and eternal, with verses of Scripture to prove this.

5. What is the difference between God's mercy and His grace? Refer to Ephesians 2.4 & 2.8; also Titus 3.5 & 3.7.

POINTS TO REMEMBER

*   Justification means that God Himself declares or announces that a sinner is righteous when that sinner believes in the Lord Jesus.
*   Only God, the righteous Judge, can justify anyone.
*   The blood of Christ shed on the cross is the righteous basis for our justification.
*   The grace of God is the source of our justification and the only way by which we could obtain it.
*   Our personal faith in Christ is essential for us to be justified.
*   Once we are saved, others should see our good works which demonstrate that we are believers.
*   We are justified by faith before God, and justified by works before men.

CHAPTER 7

Sanctified

Many times in the New Testament, believers in Christ are called *saints*. Almost every epistle written by Paul to a church is addressed to the saints in that place - see Romans 1.7, Colossians 1.2, and the first verses in 2 Corinthians, Ephesians, and Philippians.

We usually think that the word "saint" refers to someone who is specially holy. But it really means someone whom God has **specially set apart** for Himself. They are set apart from sin and their former life, and set apart to be God's own people. Therefore they should be holy. Every believer is set apart in this way when they trust Christ for salvation.

To be **sanctified** means to be set apart for God, to be made and called a saint. This **sanctification** is the work of God. So we read that the church of God at Corinth is made up of those "are *sanctified* in Christ Jesus, and called *saints*" (1 Corinthians 1.2). Also at Thessalonica, "God has chosen you to salvation through *sanctification* of the Spirit and belief of the truth" (2 Thessalonians 2.13).

There are two sides to our sanctification.

1. What God has already done for us
We have been "sanctified by God the Father" (Jude v.1). God's work is always perfect and complete. In 1 Corinthians 6.11 we read that when sinners are saved they "are washed, sanctified, and justified in the name of the Lord Jesus". Also "we are sanctified by the offering of the body of Jesus Christ once for all" (Hebrews 10.10).

Christ is the "Sanctifier" and the believers are "the sanctified", and they are "all of one" (Hebrews 2.11). This means that there is a wonderful union between Christ and His people. This union was shown when He said, "I ascend to my Father, and your Father, to my God, and your God" (John 20.17). Also we read, "Christ Jesus, who of God is made unto us wisdom, and righteousness, and sanctification, and redemption" (1 Corinthians 1.30). Apart from Christ we could not be redeemed or sanctified, but in Him we have sanctification along with redemption.

This sanctification becomes ours by faith. The Lord Jesus said that we would receive "forgiveness of sins, and an inheritance among them which are sanctified by faith that is in Me" (Acts 26.18). We noticed in chapter 6 that we are "justified by His blood" (Romans 5.9). In the same way we are "sanctified by His own blood" (Hebrews 13.12). By the work of the Cross, *we are perfectly justified and perfectly sanctified once for all*. We now have "an inheritance among all them who are sanctified" (Acts 20.32).

God has sanctified us to Himself. That means we are *set apart for a special and higher purpose*. That purpose is to make us His own people. We can call Him Father, and we can now worship Him in the heavenly sanctuary. He has given us fitness to enter into that holy place at any time.

2. What God is continually doing in us

In 1 Thessalonians 5.23 we read the following prayer: "The very God of peace sanctify you wholly". Also the Lord Jesus prayed: "Sanctify them through Thy truth; Thy Word is truth" (John 17.17). This shows us that God wants to bring about our sanctification more and more each day. He wants us to be "a vessel sanctified", fit for the Master's use (2 Timothy 2.21). He wants to sanctify us "wholly".

This is something which all believers should desire to be. But the old life (the old nature) which remains in us hinders us from reaching it completely. It will not be easy. Our daily and practical *sanctification is an ongoing process.* We can never think that we are sanctified enough. Each of us should be growing more and more like Christ.

What God has made us should have a practical effect on the way we live.

- Since God has made us saints, we should live saintly, holy lives.
- Since God has set us apart for Himself, we should ourselves be separate from sin and evil.
- Our sanctified position before God should lead to sanctified living every day.
- Because He is holy, we should be holy too (1 Peter 1.16).

In the books of Exodus and Leviticus, we read about priests who brought sacrifices to God in the tabernacle. They were specially set apart by God for this work, sanctified and chosen from among the other Israelites for this sacred task (Exodus 28.41). But when they came in to the tabernacle, they had to be clean to do their work for God. So they washed their hands and feet at a large basin called the laver which stood in the court (30.17-21). In the same way Christians must daily cleanse their ways by the Word of God (Psalm 119.9), and be separate from everything that would defile and spoil them for the presence and service of God. We always need to cleanse ourselves "from all filthiness of flesh and spirit" (2 Corinthians 7.2). We should be separate from 'unequal yokes' or alliances with unbelievers (2 Corinthians 6.14-17), and also from teachers of evil doctrine (2 Timothy 2.21).

It is very important to live a life which is in keeping with the position God has given us. We must show practically that we are sanctified. The Corinthian believers were "sanctified in Christ Jesus" (1 Corinthians

1.2). But as you read more about them you find that they were not living like that. In that church, sin was being allowed, it was not being judged or put away. They were dishonouring God and their holy calling. So in 1 Corinthians 5 they are called to put away evil because of their sanctified position.

The believer is now in Christ. He or she is one of the "holy brethren, partakers of the heavenly calling" (Hebrews 3.1), placed in a position of nearness to God. We are worshippers in His sanctuary, servants doing His work, and children in His family. Therefore we must avoid everything which does not match this place into which His grace has brought us. We must "lay aside every weight, and the sin which so easily besets us" and make progress as we "run with patience the race which is set before us." (Hebrews 12.1).

QUESTIONS

1. *The Bible speaks of Christ Himself being sanctified. What does this mean?*

   In John 10.36 we read that Christ is the One "whom the Father has sanctified and sent into the world". This cannot mean that He was made more holy, for He always was and is completely holy. Remember that the meaning of 'sanctify' is to set apart for a special purpose. So the verse means that our Lord was set apart by God to be His perfect servant on earth, and to become the perfect sacrifice for sin. See also John 17.19.

2. *What does 'sanctified' mean in the Old Testament?*

   God "blessed the seventh day and sanctified it" (Genesis 2.3), that is, He set it apart as a day of rest. It was still a day, the same length as other days, but it was set apart by God for a special purpose. The first-born of men and beasts were sanctified (Exodus 13.2), set apart for God. The brass altar in the tabernacle and the garments of the priests were sanctified (Exodus 29.44; 28.2). They were made of ordinary materials, but they were selected for a higher use and purpose. In the same way, Christians are ordinary men and women who have been chosen and set apart for God's pleasure and purpose.

3. *Will believers ever be perfectly holy in this life - experiencing a "complete sanctification"?*

   We will never be totally sinless or perfectly holy in this life. Our old nature will always drag us away from godliness and holiness. Read Romans 7.14-25 to see the struggle which Paul had with the old nature, and this is what we all experience. Neither penance on one hand, or a superior spiritual experience on the other, will deliver us from "the flesh" and its tendency to take us away from the will of God. Only when we reach heaven will we be perfect in every way.

FOR FURTHER STUDY

1. Explain how a person becomes a saint, with verses from the New Testament to prove it.

2. What aspect of sanctification is referred to in 1 Thessalonians 4.3, and how is it achieved?

3. Read John 17.19 and explain how first the Lord Jesus, and then His people, would be "sanctified".

4. Explain the difference between 'separation' and 'sanctification', and explain how both are necessary for us.

POINTS TO REMEMBER

- To be sanctified means to be set apart for God, to be a holy people, separate from all kinds of evil.
- Sanctification has two parts (1) what God did for us when we were saved, and (2) what we must allow God to do for us more and more throughout our lives.
- The blood of Christ has sanctified us completely.
- The Word of God will sanctify us continuously.
- Others should notice that we are a holy and separated people.

CHAPTER 8

Eternal Life

Eternal life is the same as everlasting life, spoken of about forty five times in the New Testament. Those who put their trust in Christ for salvation possess eternal life. By nature, man is spiritually dead, but when a person is born again, they pass from death into life (John 5.24). "The wages of sin is death, but *the gift of God is eternal life* through Jesus Christ our Lord" (Romans 6.23).

What is eternal life?

Eternal life is not just "living for ever" after you die. Actually, every person will live for ever, but every person will not have eternal life. The human soul has an endless existence. It does not die when the body dies. The body will be raised from the dead one day and reunited with the soul. The Bible tells us that believers will enjoy the bliss of heaven, and unbelievers will endure the torment of the lake of fire, for ever (Revelation 21.7-8).

Everyone will have a conscious existence after death. The words of the Lord Jesus in Luke 16.19-31 show this very clearly. The rich man lifted up his eyes being in torments. He was conscious, and in pain. He could remember his former life. He could request somebody to be sent to warn his family. But there was a great space that no one could cross. In eternity the unbeliever will exist, but they will not "see life" (John 3.36). They will rather endure the "second death" (Revelation 20.14-15), which is an endless existence of suffering and separation from God.

Some people say that man is just like a beast at death and does not live on to meet God in eternity. Some say that Ecclesiastes 3.19-22 shows this. But this contradicts the clear teaching of Scripture that *man is different*: "God breathed into man the breath of life and man became a living soul" (Genesis 2.7). This is not said about the animals. Man was made in the image of God, created separate from animals (Genesis 1.26).

These verses in Ecclesiastes are in a book which tells us about a man's search for wisdom. The writer asks questions and tries to find answers, but his knowledge was not perfect, and his conclusions were not final. These verses do *not* mean that man and animals are the same. The only similarity is that their bodies die, that is all. Psalm 49.20 also speaks of man being "like beasts that perish". Again, this refers to death of the body, not of the soul. A beast perishes without any hope or future. A man who does not understand his need of God also has no hope. But that does not mean that his soul ceases to live after death. Other verses in the Bible teach clearly that man's soul lives on into eternity.

So what is eternal life? It is a new state of wonderful blessing and privilege which God gives **here and now** to those who trust His Son as Saviour. The important thing about eternal life is its quality rather than its duration. It is spiritual, not natural. It comes from God, not man. From our human links with Adam we inherit death. We were "dead in trespasses and sins" (Ephesians 2.1). But our Lord Jesus Christ came and died for us so that we could have eternal life, which is God's life put into our souls.

The wonderful blessing of eternal life is obtained only through faith in Christ: "Whosoever *believes* in Him should not perish but *have eternal life*" (John 3.15). Jesus said, "I am come that they might have life, and that they might have it more abundantly" (John 10.10). "Abundantly" means that the life which Christ gives is the best kind of life which anyone can have. It is something quite different from our natural life and much superior to it. In fact to miss receiving eternal life is to miss the greatest blessing you could ever receive in this world. Sadly the

Lord Jesus had to say to some people one day, "You will not come to me that you might have life" (John 5.40).

When does eternal life begin?

Eternal life does not begin after a believer dies. It begins whenever a person trusts Christ for salvation. That person at once receives eternal life within their soul. It is a present possession, as the words of the Lord Jesus show clearly: "He that hears My word and believes in Him that sent me, *has everlasting life*, and shall not come into judgement, but *is passed from death into life*." (John 5.24). This is not a promise of life to come later. It is a gift of life which begins *now.*

Everyone is born into this world with natural life. This can be seen in the physical and mental development of a growing child. In the same way eternal life begins when a person is born again, and this spiritual life will be seen by others as the believer grows in grace. If we have God's life in us, we grow and learn by feeding on the "milk of the Word" (1 Peter 2.2). In 1 John 2.12-13 we read about different stages in the development of God's people, from children to young men to fathers. They have different experiences of God and of living for Him. But all possess equally that eternal life which they were given when they trusted in Christ. "These things have I written unto you that believe on the name of the Son of God; that you may know that *you have eternal life*" (1 John 5.13).

Can eternal life be lost?

Anything which is eternal or everlasting cannot be ended or lost. If it were, it would not be eternal. Thus the *eternal life of a believer will not be interrupted by death*. It will continue in a better place called heaven. In our mortal bodies here the enjoyment of our eternal life is very often restricted and its expression is incomplete. The weakness and frailty of these "earthen vessels" (2 Corinthians 4.7) and these "earthly tents" (5.1-4) sometimes prevent the full enjoyment of spiritual things. The life is within us, but its fullness is not known. When we reach heaven and have a new body to live in, the full joy and expression of eternal life will then be possible (Philippians 3.20-21). So while we are here on earth we look forward to something more. We are "looking for the mercy of our Lord Jesus Christ unto eternal life" (Jude v. 21).

Also the *eternal life of a believer cannot be lost due to anything which might happen here on earth*. The Lord Jesus said, "I give to them eternal life, and they shall never perish" (John 10.28). "Never" means never! Not in this world or the next! Our salvation is eternal because it does not depend upon us but only upon Christ. He will never allow any soul which has trusted Him to perish or be lost. To emphasise this, Jesus added that no one can "pluck them out of My hand. My Father which gave them Me is greater than all; and no one is able to pluck them out of My Father's hand" (v. 29). When a person is born again they receive eternal life from God. This verse tells us that they can never lose it.

Eternal life is to know "the only true God, and Jesus Christ whom Thou hast sent" (John 19.2-3). We trust Him and know Him as Saviour now, and we will go on to know Him more and more for ever. Because eternal life depends on what Christ has done, He Himself is called "that eternal life which was with the Father and was manifested to us" (1 John 1.2). In Christ we possess eternal life. Out of Christ we have nothing. It is wonderful to be able to say, "We are in Him that is true, even in His Son Jesus Christ; this is the true God and eternal life" (1 John 5.20).

QUESTIONS

1. *What does it mean to "perish" as in John 3.16?*

   This is the opposite of having eternal life. It does not mean loss of being, but loss of well-being; it is not destruction, but separation from God and from all that is good for ever. It is the terrible fate of those who will not believe. Remember that God is not willing that any should perish (2 Peter 3.9), but alas many choose that way for themselves by refusing the gospel of Christ.

2. *What happens to the body, the soul and the spirit when someone dies?*

   The *body* is mortal and corruptible (1 Corinthians 15.53), which means that when life is over its structure decomposes. That is why we bury bodies.
   The *soul* is the real person who lives in the body. The soul lives on, in heaven for the believer - "absent from the body, present with the Lord" (2 Corinthians 5.8); in hell for the unbeliever - "tormented" (Luke 16.23-25).
   The *spirit*, the "breath of life" which God first breathed into man at creation (Genesis 2.7) returns to God who gave it (Ecclesiastes 12.7).
   The body will be raised again from the dead, changed from being corruptible to being incorruptible, and reunited with the soul. For believers this will happen when the Lord Jesus comes again (1 Corinthians 15.51-54).

3. *Do the spirits of dead people return to earth, to where they used to live?*

   No. The spirit of any person, believer or unbeliever, belongs to God. After they die, He retains it in His own power. The only spirits on earth are (1) the Holy Spirit which God gives to dwell in each believer when they are converted; and (2) evil spirits from Satan which do influence people on earth to lead them away from God.

4. *Is it possible to contact the spirits of the dead?*

Some people pretend to be in touch with the spirits of the dead. You must remember that these people make money by the results they get, therefore, the more convincing they can be the better their reputation and the more money they can make.

The Bible forbids dealing with a medium, a witch, or anyone who has a 'familiar spirit' (Leviticus 19.31; 20.6). It is wrong to turn to these people for help, because the spirits which they contact are not those of the dead, but are in fact evil spirits. In 1 Samuel 28.7-14 we read about king Saul going to the witch of Endor to try to get in touch with Samuel who had died. She knew as soon as she had called up the spirit of Samuel that this was different from what normally happened when she called up the spirits. In this case God had brought back the spirit of Samuel to teach Saul a lesson. These spirits are liars and deceivers (1 Kings 22.22-23; John 8.44), so we should not believe anything which they say.

5. *Is it possible for a Christian to be possessed by a demon?*

When someone believes in Christ now, and therefore becomes a Christian, God delivers them from the power of darkness and transfers them into the kingdom of His Son (Colossians 1.13). Christians cannot be possessed by an evil spirit because they have the Holy Spirit dwelling in them.

The Bible does not say how or why any person becomes possessed by a demon. Such people could not be part of God's holy community in the Old Testament. The Law said that they had to be put to death (Exodus 22.18; Leviticus 20.27). When the Lord Jesus was on earth, one of the proofs of His presence was that the demons recognised Him (for example Matthew 8.28-29). He taught that first the strong man (Satan) had to be bound so that his goods (people) could be released from his ownership (Matthew 12.28-29), and so the Lord Jesus cast out many demons. The kingdom of God had come in the person of the Lord Jesus Christ and it was the stronger kingdom.

6. *Do evil spirits cause people to sin?*

   Spirits can deceive and give much trouble, but they cannot cause people to sin. Sin is an act of man's own will.

FOR FURTHER STUDY

1. What is the difference between physical life and spiritual life?

2. What is the difference between immortality which everyone has, and eternal life which only believers in Christ have?

3. Many different things in the Bible are said to be "eternal". Here are just a few of them: eternal God, eternal glory, eternal salvation, eternal fire. Try to find some others.

4. Explain how eternal life is both present and future for the believer.

POINTS TO REMEMBER

- Eternal life is the same as everlasting life which is the gift of God to everyone who trusts in Christ for salvation. But it is not the same as immortality which everyone has.
- Eternal life begins when a person trusts in Christ and is saved. It can be enjoyed here and now, and it cannot be lost for any reason.
- Different things happen to the body, the soul, and the spirit when a person dies. The soul is the real person which lives on in eternity.

CHAPTER 9

Assurance of Salvation

Can we be sure of having eternal life?

We read in the Bible, "These things have I written to you that believe on the name of the Son of God; that you may *know* that you have eternal life" (1 John 5.13).

God wants us to be saved, and to know it. He wants us to be sure that we are saved. Assurance is simply this - *knowing and being sure that you are saved.*

Remember that we did not save ourselves. If we had to try to save ourselves we could never be sure about how safe and secure we would be! But it is God that saves us (Titus 3.5), and so there is no cause for any doubts at all. We can be sure about what God does.

- Our salvation depends on the work of Christ being complete, and we know that this work is complete, for He cried, "It is finished!" (John 19.30).
- Our assurance depends on the Word of God being true and reliable, and we know that His Word is reliable, for Jesus said, "Heaven and earth shall pass away, but My words shall never pass away" (Matthew 24.35).
- We are *saved* because Christ died for us. Our salvation rests on the precious blood of Christ.
- We are *sure* because God says so. Our assurance rests on the unchanging Word of God.

Being saved and being sure

If a person is not saved, it is because they have not accepted Christ as

Saviour and put their trust in Him. If a person is not *sure* of salvation, it is because they have not really believed what God has said in His Word. In that Word we read, "He that believes on the Son *has* everlasting life" (John 3.36); "All that believe *are* justified from all things" (Acts 13.39). God would not say such things unless they were true!

If you are unsure of having eternal life you are really saying, "I cannot take God's Word for it. I cannot believe that I am saved just because God says it."

Here is what some people do:

- They look for signs. But faith trusts God without signs.
- They want to understand all about it, to reason it out, and then believe. But faith accepts what God says. It is "by *faith* that we *understand*" (Hebrews 11.3), not by understanding we obtain faith.
- They look for evidences in their lives. But the assurance of salvation is not obtained by becoming holy or achieving spiritual greatness.
- They say that they do not feel saved. But our feelings change, they go up and down and are very undependable. We are not saved because we might feel saved, but because the finished work of Christ and the testimony of God's Word are *absolutely dependable* all the time and *guarantee* that we are saved.

What God says

The Scriptures tell us clearly what we *are,* what we *have,* what we *know,* and what we *shall be,* so that we can be sure. The following facts are true for all who believe in the Lord Jesus. They are written for our assurance in the Word of God. You should read these verses for yourself, and remember that it is all true *because God says so.*

- *We are -*

  saved (1 Corinthians 1.18); forgiven (1 John 2.12); washed; sanctified; justified (1 Corinthians 6.11); sons or children of God (1 John 3.1); complete in Christ (Colossians 2.10).

- *We have -*

  redemption (Ephesians 1.7); peace (Romans 5.1); eternal life (John 3.14); the Holy Spirit (1 Corinthians 2.12); a Great High Priest (Hebrews 8.1); an Advocate with the Father (1 John 2.2).

- *We know -*

  we are of God (1 John 5.19); we have passed from death into life (3.14); we are of the truth (3.19); we are in Him (2.5); we have eternal life (5.11); we have a home in heaven (2 Corinthians 5.1).

- *We shall be -*

  raised (1 Thessalonians 4.16); changed (1 Corinthians 15.52); caught up to meet the Lord in the air (1 Thessalonians 4.17); like Him (1 John 3.2); with Him (1 Thessalonians 4.17); satisfied in His presence for ever (Psalm 17.15).

It is normal to be sure of having eternal life?

To have the assurance of salvation and to rejoice in it is normal for every believer in Christ. Paul wrote to the believers, "Our Gospel came not unto you in word only, but in power, and in the Holy Spirit, and in *much assurance*" (1 Thessalonians 1.5). To lack this assurance can be the result of unbelief in God's Word (1 John 5.10), or the result of traditional and false teaching (Galatians 3.1; 4.9), or the result of backsliding (2 Peter 1.9).

There are many helpful pictures of assurance in the Bible.

- Noah believed God about a coming flood (Genesis 6.13-17). He had the assurance that a flood was coming one hundred and twenty years before it came. He knew it, and preached about it, because he believed God.

- "Abraham believed God" (Romans 4.2) when He promised to give him a son. The evidences were all against it, but he "was strong in faith … being fully persuaded that what He had promised He was able also to perform" (v. 21). He had the assurance of receiving a son, long before Isaac was born.

- The Israelites in Egypt were safe when the blood had been applied to the doorposts of their houses. They had the assurance of their safety because God had said, "I will pass over you" (Exodus 12.13). Their safety depended on their obedience to God. But their assurance depended on their confidence in His Word. If they simply believed what God said, then they could say, "We are safe, because God has said it." If, however, they looked inside themselves at their feelings, they could be very uncertain and afraid. Similarly, many people now look within themselves, seeking for evidences of assurance there. Of course they are disappointed. There can be no assurance apart from resting your faith on what God has said.

Job had assurance (Job 19.25); so had David (Psalm 103.12), and Isaiah (Isaiah 6.7). In the New Testament, so had Paul (2 Corinthians 5.1), John (1 John 3.2), Timothy (2 Timothy 1.9), Peter (1 Peter 5.1), all the believers at Ephesus (Ephesians 1.7) at Colosse (Colossians 1.12-14), and other churches.

Read these verses again and you will see that the normal thing for all believers, long ago and today, is to *know* that they are saved and possess eternal life.

QUESTIONS

1. *Is it possible to be a believer, and yet to lack the assurance of salvation?*

   The Scriptures clearly state that all who believe on the Son of God *have* everlasting life. This fact cannot be altered. The *possession* of eternal life does not depend on what we know or feel. However, the *enjoyment* of it does. Some people have life but also have many doubts and fears. Some might even think that these doubts and fears are certain 'marks of grace', and that they should always examine themselves to find 'evidences' of their Christianity. That is not the way to get assurance of salvation. Assurance comes by just trusting God.

2. *Was Paul afraid of being lost, when he spoke of being a "castaway" in 1 Corinthians 9.27?*

   No, salvation is not the subject here, but service and its reward. Paul was always confident about his salvation, because that was in the Lord's hands. But the ministry or service that the Lord had committed to him was in his own hands. Like a runner in the games, he might miss the prize. The running, fighting, and self-discipline mentioned in v.26-27 were to obtain a crown, not to obtain salvation. Life is the gift of God (Romans 6.23); "the crown of life" is a reward for service here (Revelation 2.10).

3. *Do the words of Hebrews 6.4-7 apply to believers?*

   No! True believers cannot "fall away" and "perish". This is clearly taught in John 10.28. The verses in Hebrews 6 are specifically about those Jews who had seen the "powers of the age to come" at Pentecost, when miracles and signs had been given. If they turned their back upon all they had heard and seen, refusing salvation, there was no salvation for them. No born again person ever did that. It is possible for a sinner to be "enlightened" and yet never to have been born again.

FOR FURTHER STUDY

1. It has always been the work of Satan to make people doubt the Word of God, and rob them of their confidence in God. Read about this in Genesis 3.1, and then think of other examples.

2. In 2 Timothy 1.12, Paul speaks very confidently about his salvation and his future. Why do you think he can do this? Can you do the same?

3. Read 1 John 3.18-21 and note that how we live and what we do, give us a clear conscience before God. How does this match our assurance of having eternal life?

POINTS TO REMEMBER

* From God's Word we receive the assurance of being saved.
* God's Word and His promises are totally true and can be trusted.
* It is normal and necessary for Christians to be sure of their own salvation.
* God does not want us to doubt Him, but to rest in peace upon His Word.
* Our feelings change and can deceive us. God's Word never changes. Always trust in what God has said.

CHAPTER 10

Judgement

Many people do not like to hear about judgement. It is very unpopular and unwelcome because it means they will have to give account of what they have done, and perhaps face punishment. Some modern teaching tries to deny that there is any future judgement to worry about. Many welcome this because they think they can live as they please without any fear of the consequences of their actions.

But you cannot read the Bible without discovering that *there certainly is a judgement*. In fact God has given us His Word so that we might know how to be prepared for the judgement, and escape the punishment we deserve. God's warnings are just as important as His promises. They must be taken seriously.

So we read –

- "It is appointed to men once to die, but after this the judgement" (Hebrews 11.27).
- God "has appointed a day in which He will judge the world" (Acts 17.31).
- There will be a "day of wrath and revelation of the righteous judgement of God" (Romans 2.5).
- "God will bring you into judgement" (Ecclesiastes 11.9).

At this point there are two important things to note.

1. The judgement will be absolutely *fair and just*. There will be no mistakes made, nothing overlooked. "Shall not the Judge of all the earth do right?" (Genesis 18.25). Human judges sometimes make mistakes but God's judgement is always just (John 5.30).

2. Those who have done what God has required of them have *nothing to fear* from the judgement. The same judgement which condemns those who are guilty, approves and protects those who have done what is right.

In the Bible we read of different judgements for different types of people. It is important to distinguish them and understand why each is necessary in the plans which God has for the future. We will look at these now.

1. The Future Judgement of Unbelievers

This is very solemnly described in Revelation 20.11-15. God's **Great White Throne** of Judgement is set up. All who have ever lived and died in their sins are judged according to their works, and those who are not in the Book of Life are cast into the lake of fire. There is no escape from the judgement of God upon sin which has not been forgiven (Romans 2.3). In this world sometimes wicked criminals escape the judgement and punishment for their wrong doing. No one will escape the righteous judgement of God.

Sinners are "condemned already" if they do not believe on the Lord Jesus Christ (John 3.18). By coming to Christ in faith for salvation, their sins can be taken away, they can be justified. But if they do not come, and they "die in their sins: where I go you cannot come," Jesus said (John 8.21). This is very sad, because God wants all to be saved (1 Timothy 2.4); He wants no one to perish (2 Peter 3.9).

The great gospel promise from Christ Himself is "He that hears My word, and believes on Him that sent me, has everlasting life and shall not come into judgement (condemnation); but is passed from death into life" (John 5.24). The second death, which is hell and the lake of fire (Revelation 20.14; 21.8), is God's punishment for those who refuse His offer of salvation. It is very serious. This judgement and punishment is eternal - the Lord Jesus Himself said, "These shall go away into everlasting punishment: but the righteous into life eternal" (Matthew 25.46).

Those who preach the Gospel should remember to give warnings about the coming judgement, telling people, as John Baptist did long ago, to "flee from the wrath to come" (Matthew 3.7). The "day of salvation" is now (2 Corinthians 6.2) but "the day of judgement" is coming when those who have rejected salvation will be punished (2 Peter 2.9).

2. The Judgement of Believers

For a believer in Christ there are three types of judgement described in the Bible. One is past, one is present, and the other is future.

Past Judgement - as a sinner at God's throne

The judgement for a believer's sins is past and gone. On the cross at Calvary, our Lord Jesus Christ took all the judgement and punishment which was due to us. The justice of God assures us that because our Saviour bore our judgement it will not fall on us. The price of our sin has been paid by the precious blood of Christ (1 Peter 1.18) and will not need to be paid again. "He bore our sins in His own body on the tree" (1 Peter 2.24). Therefore we are free and justified before God. We can say, "I have been crucified with Christ" (Galatians 2.20).

The believer is **completely delivered** from the "judgement to come". There will be many judgements, judgements of the living, and of the dead; some in time (Matthew 25.31), some in eternity (Revelation 20.11). But whatever they are, God says that the believer will not come into judgement because of their sin (John 5.24). Indeed, we can "have boldness in the day of judgement" because we are in Christ for whom all judgement is past (1 John 4.17). For the believer in Christ the future holds no terrors or fears. His "perfect love casts out fear" (1 John 4.18).

Present Judgement - as a child in God's family

The believer in Christ is no longer a sinner waiting for judgement to come. He is in God's family, subject to God's **rule and discipline**, such as every true father exercises within his family (Hebrews 12.6-9). We are "the children of God by faith in Christ Jesus" (Galatians 3.26).

God as a Father expects His children to obey Him (1 Peter 1.14). Obedient children receive their Father's approval (Hebrews 11.6) and enjoy His fellowship (John 14.23). But those who are disobedient are corrected by His Word (John 15.3) and also by His discipline (Hebrews 12.5). If a believer sins, fellowship with the Father is broken. When sin is confessed and forsaken, fellowship is restored (1 John 1.9). If sin is not confessed, our Father in His wisdom brings in discipline, for our profit (Hebrews 12.10). The judgement of God's children is not to condemn them but to correct them and enable to enjoy their true place in His family.

King David found out to his great sorrow and loss that disobedience to God and sin against God brought severe pain and discipline until he repented and confessed it all (Psalm 51.1-4; 32.3-5). If we should judge ourselves and forsake our own sin, God will not have to judge us and correct us in this way (1 Corinthians 11.31-32).

Future Judgement - as a servant in God's work

Every believer is called to be a servant of the Lord Jesus, put in trust with his Master's goods (read Matthew 25.14-15). We have been called to a life of service for our absent Master (Mark 13.34). When He returns, our service will be reviewed and rewarded (see Luke 19.12-27, especially v.15). "Every one of us shall give account of himself to God" (Romans 14.12). "We must all appear before the Judgement Seat of Christ" (2 Corinthians 5.10). This is where our service will be carefully and properly **assessed and rewarded** by the Lord Himself.

This **"Judgement Seat"** is not a place for punishment, but for reward. It is not like a law court, but rather is like the place where a judge watches a contest or a race, and then rewards the winners who have kept the rules. The Lord Jesus is presently watching our efforts in the race of life (Hebrews 12.1-2); also our works in the church and elsewhere (Revelation 2.2). He sees and notes what we do and why we do it. When we appear before Him He will give His "well done" for everything which has pleased and honoured Him.

- He will consider how well or how carelessly we treated our brothers and sisters in Christ (Romans 14.10).
- He will consider the things we have done with our bodies, whether good or bad (2 Corinthians 5.10).
- What we built into our local church will be "tried with fire" (1 Corinthians 3.11-15) to see what is of lasting value.

All this brings a great challenge to us now, because what we do now will determine what reward we will receive then. This surely encourages us to live and work for Christ to the very best of our ability.

Rewards will be different for each believer, according to their faithfulness and the type of work they did. There will be a "crown of life" (Revelation 2.10), a "crown of righteousness" (2 Timothy 4.8), a "crown of rejoicing" (1 Thessalonians 2.19), and a "crown of glory" (1 Peter 5.4). The word from the Lord to each of us just now, before He comes again, is, "Hold fast that which you have, so that no one takes your crown" (Revelation 3.11). He says, "Behold I come quickly; and My reward is with Me, to give to every man *according as his work shall be*" (Revelation 22.12).

After King David had received the throne and the kingdom of Israel, one of the first things he did was to reward those who had served him while he was being rejected, according to their faithfulness to him (2 Samuel 23). He gave to them the honour of high places in his kingdom. In the same way the Lord Jesus in heaven will reward those faithful ones who have served Him and suffered for His Name while He was rejected on earth. "If we suffer, we shall reign with Him: if we deny Him, He also will deny us" (2 Timothy 2.12).

QUESTIONS

1. *How will God judge those who have never heard the gospel?*

    The testimony of creation and of conscience is given to all. Romans 1.19-20; 2.15-16 tells us that God will take that into account in the day of judgement. We can be sure that all God's judgements are just and perfect. He always judges people by the light they have received from Him.

    This question is difficult to answer, and the full answer is not given in Scripture. But this must not be used as an excuse by anyone who *has* heard the gospel for not believing what *they* have heard.

2. *Will the sins of believers be dealt with at the Judgement Seat of Christ?*

    No. They were dealt with when Christ died on the cross. God says He will remember His people's sins no more (Hebrews 8.12). The blood of Christ cleanses us from all sin (1 John 1.7). A believer's sin can make his service ineffective, and he will thus lose reward (1 Corinthians 3.15). But the Judgement Seat does not consider punishment for sin. It considers reward for service.

3. *In what sense can a Christian eat and drink damnation, as we read in 1 Corinthians 11.29?*

The word 'damnation' is better translated 'judgement'. It does not mean eternal condemnation. The context shows that the 'judgement' is the present dealings of the Lord with His own people who are continuing to do what dishonours Him, unwilling to judge themselves. Illness, weakness, and even death, could happen to them. But even in its severest form, it does not condemn them "with the world" (v. 32).

FOR FURTHER STUDY

1. Read Acts 24.24-25 and note what it was that made Felix tremble. Why do you think he was afraid, but did not repent?

2. What judgement is referred to in 2 Timothy 4.1?

3. In Matthew 7.1-2 and in 1 Corinthians 4.5, we are told not to judge others. Why is this? But we are expected to judge some matters - what are these? (See for example 1 Corinthians 6.2,5, and Exodus 18.21-22.)

4. Read Deuteronomy 16.18-20 and see that God expects men to judge others with fairness and justice. Notice that this is true of God Himself, as Romans 2.5-11 will show you.

5. According to John 3.18 and John 16.9, what is the greatest sin for which anyone will be judged?

6. At the Great White Throne (Revelation 20.11-15) the judgement is based upon two things. What are they? (see v.13 and v.15).

7. Note that judgement means approving what is right and condemning what is wrong - giving praise for doing right and

punishment for doing wrong. Find Bible verses (some are given in this chapter) which speak of both types of judgement.

POINTS TO REMEMBER

- God is a God of justice and judgement. He will approve what is right and punish what is wrong.
- Judgement upon sin and sinners will take place after death at the Great White Throne of God. It will result in the punishment of the lake of fire.
- Christ bore God's judgement upon sin at the cross, so that all who accept Him and trust in Him for salvation will not face judgement and punishment for their sins.
- Believers in Christ may experience God's discipline in their lifetime as a result of their disobedience to Him, but they will not be condemned or expelled from God's family.
- At the Judgement Seat of Christ every believer will give an account of their life and service for God and receive rewards for their own faithfulness to Him on earth.

CHAPTER 11

The Death of Christ

The death of our Lord Jesus Christ is the central truth of the Gospel. Without it there would be no Gospel to preach. There would be no salvation for sinners. Many Old Testament happenings, symbols and ceremonies pointed forward to it, and the blessings described in the New Testament result from it. It was in the plan of God from before the world began, and throughout the future ages everyone in heaven will look back upon it with praise and thanksgiving.

A large part of each of the four Gospels is taken up with the events surrounding the death of Christ. In these Gospels, the records of His birth and His life, His work and His teachings are all very important. We admire and learn from the whole of His three and a half years of service to God and man. But the Holy Spirit through the Gospel writers wishes to draw more of our attention to His death and all that it means. Let us see why His death is of so great importance.

First, four different words and phrases are used in the New Testament to describe the death of our Lord. They are very significant and each has a slightly different meaning. They are –

- the cross of Christ
- the blood of Christ
- the sufferings of Christ
- the death of Christ

   (a) We read about the **"Cross of Christ"**, or simply **"the Cross"**, almost thirty times in the Gospels and the Epistles. Almost another fifty times we read the word "crucified" which means being nailed to a cross.

The **Cross** reminds us of the ***hatred of the world*** towards Him. "They crucified Him" is stated in all four Gospels. To crucify the Son of God is the worst crime of the human race. It also tells of the extreme devotion and humiliation of our Saviour. Crucifixion was the most awful and degrading way to be put to death, but He chose that way, "even the death of *the cross*" (Philippians 2.8). The crucifixion of our Saviour is still misunderstood by many. It is sometimes thought of as a great mistake, as Scripture tells us: "the preaching of *the cross* is to them that perish foolishness; but to us who are saved it is the power of God" (1 Corinthians 1.18). But we must continue to "preach Christ *crucified*" (1 Corinthians 1.23).

(b) We often speak about and read about the **"Blood of Christ"**. It is referred to at least twenty five times between Acts and Revelation.

The **"blood of Christ"** shed on the cross shows to all that the ***requirements of a holy God have been met***. Therefore He can pardon the guilty sinner who believes in Jesus (Romans 3.25-26). Hebrews 9.22 states that "without the *shedding of blood*, there is no remission of sins". The Lord Jesus Himself spoke of "*My blood* which is shed for you" (Luke 22.20), "for the remission of sins" (Matthew 26.28). "The blood of the Lamb" is a phrase which takes us from Exodus 12 through 1 Peter 1.19 to Revelation 12.11. The Lord Jesus was identified as "the Lamb of God" who would take away the sin of the world (John 1.29). In heaven we will for ever praise Him who has "loosed us from our sins *in His own blood*" (Revelation 1.5).

Some of the verses in the New Testament referring to His blood can be better understood by looking back into the Old Testament. Especially in the book of Leviticus we read about sacrifices being offered and blood being shed to give a sinner acceptance before a holy God. But these sacrifices of animals or birds could not take away sin (Hebrews 10.4,11-12). Only the precious blood of Christ can remove and cleanse the guilt of sin (1 John 1.7). Only His blood satisfied the requirements of a holy God.

(c) When we read of the **"Sufferings of Christ"** it brings to our notice *what it cost Him* to become our Saviour.

In His life He suffered because of His own righteousness as others hated and despised Him. But on the Cross He suffered for sin, for our sin (1 Peter 3.18). He suffered from the judgement of God who "laid on Him the iniquity of us all" (Isaiah 53.6). A careful and reverent reading of Psalm 22 will show how much He felt the terrible pain and the suffering. It was all very real to Him. His sufferings were very great indeed. The Lord Jesus often taught that He had to suffer and die, and then afterwards enter into His glory (Matthew 16.21; Luke 24.26). The Old Testament prophets had also taught this clearly (1 Peter 1.11).

(d) The **Death of Christ** for sin and for sinners was planned before the foundation of the world (1 Peter 1.18-20). Then "when the fulness of the time was come, God sent forth His Son ... to redeem" (Galatians 4.4-5). So He came to fulfil God's purposes and finish the work God had given Him to do (John 3.34 and 17.4).

The **death of Christ** was for the sinner, in place of each one of us. Our sins deserved death – "the wages of sin is death" (Romans 6.23). But the Lord Jesus took our place and bore our punishment. So by His death, *the sinner's need has been met*. "While we were yet sinners, *Christ died for us*" (Romans 5.8). God can reach out in grace to save those who accept Christ as Saviour. Only when our Lord Jesus died on the cross do we hear those great words, "It is finished!" (John 19.30). Only because of His death can we be saved.

We can summarise this as follows -

* "the *cross* of Christ" reminds us of the *world's hatred against Him;*

- "the *blood* of Christ" reminds us that *God's holy requirements were met;*
- "the *sufferings* of Christ" reminds us of *how much it cost Him;*
- "the *death* of Christ" reminds us that our *need as sinners has been met.*

Now let us consider four more words which describe the wonderful blessings which the death of Christ has brought to us.

1. Substitution

The death of the Lord Jesus was in place of the guilty sinner. Christ willingly became the *substitute* to bear God's judgement upon sin on behalf of those who were condemned. As I trust in Him for salvation, I realise that He has died for me, in my place and for my sins. No one else could have done this, but He did - a sinless substitute for sinful me. *He died instead of me*. But unless I accept Him as my Saviour I cannot benefit from Him being my substitute.

We read, "He gave Himself a ransom *for all*" (1 Timothy 2.6). This means that salvation is available for all people everywhere because of His death. It was a death which God accepted *on behalf of all*. We also read that He came to "give Himself a ransom *for many*" (Mark 10.45). This means that for the many who have received Him, God accepts this death *instead of them*, and now they are free from any other judgement upon their sin. Their guilt and their sins are gone from the sight of God because Jesus Christ bore all the penalty and punishment on the lonely cross at Calvary (1 Peter 2.24). "The Son of God loved me, and gave Himself *for me*" (Galatians 2.20), said the apostle Paul, and we can say that too.

A good illustration of substitution is found in Genesis 22. Abraham had taken his son Isaac to be offered as a sacrifice to God. But Isaac was released from death when God provided to Abraham a ram to be offered "instead of his son" (v.13). The ram died as a substitute for Isaac, offered to God in his place. He could truly say, "It died in place of me." In the same way, each of us who accepts the Lord Jesus Christ as Saviour can say, "He took my place. He died for me."

2. Propitiation

This word *propitiation* occurs only four times in the Bible. It describes a very important part of the gospel. The key references are Romans 3.25 - "Christ Jesus whom God has set forth to be a *propitiation*"; 1 John 2.2 - "He is the *propitiation* for our sins"; 1 John 4.10 - "He sent His Son to be the *propitiation* for our sins"; Hebrews 2.17 - He would "make *propitiation* for the sins of the people".

These references show that our sins had to be dealt with because they offended God. He demands that sin be dealt with justly, and not simply overlooked. To a holy God, sin is serious, and He has been made angry because of it (2 Kings 17.17-18). If the requirements of His justice are not met, God must judge and punish the sinner.

But the wonderful truth is that God sent His Son to do everything which would satisfy these just and holy requirements. Christ's death has turned away God's anger against our sin because that death has satisfied all God's righteous claims. This is what **propitiation** means. It means that **God's wrath against sin was turned away from us** because it fell on Him "who bore our sins in His own body on the tree" (1 Peter 2.24). God can now be favourable to us and show His grace to those whose sin had offended Him and caused His anger.

In heathen religions, people sometimes tried to turn away the displeasure of their gods by bringing gifts to them, and try to win their favour. But in our case, we could do nothing to win God's favour or turn away His anger. Christ has done all this in His death, so that He is the propitiation for our sins. God is gracious to us because of Christ.

A picture of propitiation is found in the tabernacle described in Exodus. The top covering of the Ark of the Covenant was called "The

Mercy Seat", and God said, "There I will meet with you" (Exodus 25.21-22). That Mercy Seat was sprinkled with blood. It was the evidence that a sacrifice had been offered. Because of that sacrifice, a holy God could meet with a sinful people and be favourable to them, not condemn them.

The death of Christ has now provided an acceptable meeting place for God and man to come together. We know this because the word for *'mercy seat'* in Hebrews 9.5 is the same word as *'propitiation'* in Romans 3.25. It is also the word used by the sinful tax-collector when he prayed, "God be *merciful (a mercy-seat)* to me, the sinner" (Luke 18.13). God could reach and save that sinner and all sinners because of the death of Christ who made propitiation to God for their sins.

God's throne is a throne of righteousness. Our sin made it a throne of judgement. Christ by His death has made it a throne of grace.

3. Reconciliation

Reconciliation is the removal of everything which would keep man away from God. Because of our sin, we were enemies of God, at a great distance from Him. As sinners we could never make ourselves acceptable to God. But by confessing our sin, and obeying the words of the gospel, "Be reconciled to God" (2 Corinthians 5.20), we are "made near by the blood of Christ" (Ephesians 2.13). We have now been reconciled to God by the death of His Son (Romans 5.10-11). The blood of Christ has propitiated God and reconciled man to God. Reconciliation is *made for us* at the cross because there propitiation was *made to God.*

God's purpose in saving us is that we might be close to Him, have true fellowship with Him. To be reconciled is to be **at peace with Him**. So reconciliation is part of the gospel. It is another wonderful result of the death of Christ. We are now completely accepted by God (Colossians 1.21-22), "accepted in the Beloved" (Ephesians 1.6), who "made peace by the blood of His cross" (Colossians 1.20). Indeed "He is our peace" (Ephesians 2.14). Like the prodigal son of Luke 15.20 who returned to his father, we have received the kiss of reconciliation from our Father, and we are welcomed into His presence.

4. Atonement

The word 'atonement' is often used about the death of Christ, for example when we say that He died an atoning death. This word has two meanings, both of which are related to what we have just considered.

Firstly, it is very often taken to mean the same as *reconciliation*. God and man are brought together ('at-one') whereas before they were enemies. This is wonderfully true as we have just seen. But the word 'atonement' is really an Old Testament word, used mostly in Exodus, Leviticus and Numbers. It describes one of the results of the sacrifices offered for sin and the blood which was shed.

A very important verse is Leviticus 17.11: "it is the blood that makes an atonement for the soul". Atonement actually means *"covering"*. Before the death of Christ, God was willing to cover His people's sins by these sacrifices and the blood shed because they pointed forward to what Christ would do at the cross. Because blood was shed, their sins were covered and hidden from the judgement of God. Atonement was not the sacrifice itself but the *result* of the sacrifice offered. The "day of atonement" was a special feast in the Jewish year (Leviticus 23.26-32), when the high priest went into God's holiest presence with the blood and applied it to the Mercy Seat. Then, for another year, the sins of the people would be covered, hidden from God's holy judgement; they were atoned for (Leviticus 16.11-14).

However, for us, there is something much better than the atonement which is described in the Old Testament. In the New Testament it is *reconciliation*, and it is so much better.

- In atonement sins were covered from sight - in reconciliation sins are cancelled and remembered no more (Hebrews 8.12).
- Atonement was temporary and had to be repeated - reconciliation is eternal and done once for all (Hebrews 9.25-26; 10.11-12).
- Atonement never actually changed the sinner - reconciliation changes the sinner completely and makes him a child of God.
- Atonement accepted the sinner but never brought him near to God - reconciliation brings him right into God's presence in total acceptance.

But now secondly, 'atonement' really means the same as **propitiation**. When we say that the death of Christ made atonement for us we really mean that He has made propitiation for us. Atonement tells of the forbearance of God, holding back His anger against sin - propitiation has removed His anger for ever. It means that God can save us and accept us because that death has *completely* **removed** *our sin from God's sight*.

These wonderful truths of the New Testament are well illustrated for us in the Old Testament. But what we can enjoy is much deeper and better than what the people of the Old Testament could ever know. We owe all our blessings to the death of Christ.

QUESTIONS

1. *Did God have to be reconciled to man?*

   No, because the fault was all on man's side - man's sin had separated him from God. We were enemies in our minds by wicked works (Colossians 1.21); aliens and strangers far from God (Ephesians 2.12). We had made the distance from our side. The message of the Gospel is how Christ has removed the distance and how man can be reconciled to God.

2. *Is the word 'atonement' in the New Testament?*

It is found only in some translations in Romans 5.11, but the word there should really be 'reconciliation', since Romans 5.10-11 is all about reconciliation. The nearest equivalent word for atonement is 'propitiation'. Atonement is really an Old Testament word - it occurs there about eighty times.

3. *What is 'expiation'?*

Expiation describes the work of Christ to take away sin (John 1.29). The word 'expiation' is not found in the Bible, but it means removing the guilt of sin (*ex* means 'out of, away'). Propitiation is the work which Christ did towards God (*pro* means 'towards'), removing His wrath against sin. Expiation is the effect of His work towards us - our sin is removed.

FOR FURTHER STUDY

1. Make a list of all the results of the death of Christ which you can think of, including those in this chapter. Which affect you personally, and which are much wider?

2. Find the exact place in each of the four Gospels where the words "they crucified Him" are written.

3. Find in Galatians the references to the death (or the cross) of Christ, and in Hebrews to His blood (especially chapters 9 and 10). Notice the differences between them.

4. When Jesus was condemned to die, Barabbas was released and Jesus died in his place (Matthew 27.15-26). Could Barabbas really say, "He died for me"?

5. In the New Testament, the word 'propitiation' is related to the 'mercy seat' and the atonement made by the blood put upon it (see section 2 above). Check these words again in Romans 3.25, 1 John 2.2, 4.10, along with Hebrews 2.17 and Luke 18.13.

6. Read 1 Corinthians 15.1-23, and note how the truth of the gospel and the salvation of sinners requires both the death *and* the *resurrection* of Christ.

POINTS TO REMEMBER

- The death of Christ is the central truth of the gospel and the central theme of the Bible.
- Crucifixion was the most shameful way to die. The hatred of man to Christ was fully shown at the cross.
- The blood of Christ shed on the cross has met all the righteous demands of God's holy throne and therefore our sins can be forgiven.
- The sufferings of Christ were severe and intense. The cost of our salvation was very great indeed.
- Our Lord Jesus died as our substitute – He died in our place and for our sins.
- Propitiation for sin was made for us on the cross - God's anger has been turned away and He can now forgive and receive us.
- We have been reconciled to God by the cross - all distance and enmity has been removed.
- Atonement means covering sin from God's sight. This happened when sacrifices were offered in Old Testament times. But the sacrifice of Christ on the cross removed our sins altogether and we are reconciled to God for ever.

CHAPTER 12

After Salvation, What Next?

When you go on a journey, the first step is the most important one. Unless you take that first step, you will never go anywhere.

If you have taken the first step of faith by trusting in Christ as your own Saviour, you have started on the greatest and best journey of all - the journey from earth to heaven. One day you will be there, although many trials and difficulties may lie along the way. The Lord Jesus is with you, to help you through these trials, and He will never leave you or forsake you (Hebrews 13.5). Salvation is just the first step. A new life has started. Think of it like a journey which you will continue for the rest of your time on earth.

For this journey of your spiritual life, the Bible is your guide book, your road map. If you follow its guidance you will not lose your way or waste any of the time which God has given to you. The children of Israel wasted much time on their journey from Egypt to Canaan because they disobeyed God and did not trust Him fully. Do not be like them! You are a child of God, and now you need to know how to live for Him. As you get to know God and His ways, you will find that He will change you to be more and more like Him, "imitators of God as His dear children" (Ephesians 5.1). This is a work which God has begun in you (Philippians 1.6).

So after you are saved, what are the next steps you should take? These are clearly described in the Bible.

Two important things will always help you to make progress.

1. The Bible which is your guide book and your road map - if you

follow its guidance you will not lose your way or waste any of the time which God has given to you.

2.   The fellowship and company of other believers in a local church - if you meet regularly with them you will be encouraged and helped.

Bible study

Psalm 119.105 says, "Thy Word is a lamp to my feet, and a light to my path." Be sure to read the Word of God every day. Obey God's commands and follow the guidance it gives. You will not understand everything which you read in the Bible, but remember that the most important things in the Bible are the easiest to understand. The more difficult things can be studied later. Always ask the Lord to guide you as you read, so that you can understand His word (John 16.13).

Read all the way through a book of the Bible, so that you get the bigger picture. It is important to see verses in the context of the whole chapter and the whole book.

Take notes of what you are reading. Write down a summary of what the passage is about. Break it up into sections to help you to see what are the main points. Write down any questions which you might have, and get an older Christian to help you to find the answers.

Another helpful way to study the Bible is by choosing topics or subjects (for example, faith, or grace, or holiness), and follow what is taught about each one throughout the Bible. You will need a good concordance for this, or a Bible with references beside each verse can lead you to related texts.

Remember also that the main purpose of Bible study is not to fill your head with information. It is to fill your heart with love for Christ, to let your life be guided by what God has told us in His Word, and to follow the steps of faith and obedience revealed to you there.

Fellowship with other Christians

If you read in Acts 2.41-42, you will find steps of faith and obedience which God wants you to take after salvation. These steps will greatly benefit you, and also bring glory to God and encouragement to other believers.

- Those who were saved, were **baptised**. The Lord Jesus Himself was baptised (Matthew 3.13-17), and commanded that all His followers should also be baptised in water (Matthew 28.19-20) as an outward sign of their union with Him (Romans 6.4).

- Then they were **added to the local church** in Jerusalem. Such local churches exist all over the world, composed of believers in Christ who have taken these steps. The Lord Jesus wants His people to be together in fellowship with each other to worship and serve Him in the places where they live. It is not good for believers to be isolated.

- In that fellowship, they **continued steadfastly** in the apostles' doctrine. This doctrine is the teaching given in the New Testament about every aspect of Christian life and service for God. This teaching has not changed down through the years, and we should continue to obey it in our personal lives and in our church gatherings.

- They also continued in **breaking of bread**, and **prayers**. These are very important parts of church life in which our Lord expects us to be involved regularly. The Breaking of Bread, or the Lord's Supper (1 Corinthians 11.20-26), is to be kept every Lord's Day as our Saviour Himself requested and commanded: "This do, in remembrance of Me" (Luke 22.19-20). Public and united prayers are also vital for the progress and well being of the local church. We should always try to be at prayer meetings.

As you read on to the end of Acts 2, you will find that in their homes also these early Christians practised all that they believed. They shared what they had with those who had nothing. They lived simply and joyfully. They were united in praising God. They had an effective testimony. Others saw the change in their lives, and listened when they spoke to them about Christ.

In your home you also should read the Word of God and apply its teaching. Your family, friends, and neighbours will benefit from your influence. God's wonderful grace to you is something to share with others where you are.

If you follow these steps described in the Holy Scriptures, as you go on in your Christian life your own spiritual life will become deeper and richer, and God will be honoured and glorified in what you do.

FOR FURTHER STUDY

1. Follow through the Bible a subject like redemption, or blood, or worship. This will be easier if you can get a Bible with references beside each verse, or a concordance.

2. A book of daily readings can take you through some part of the Scriptures and help you to find the main lesson from the passage each day.

3. Make a list of the churches you read of in the New Testament. What do you think were the important things about them all?

POINTS TO REMEMBER

- Regular reading and study of the Bible is necessary for our spiritual progress.
- We should be part of a local church fellowship to benefit from the help of other Christians and also to be a help to them.

Index